AFRICA by INSPIRATION
A Journey through Southern Africa

Bruce Mortimer

Introduction	9
Abandoned	16
Pursuit	28
Thirst	41
Water	65
Growth	78
Limit	102
Summit	128
Nurture	140
Acknowledgements	178

Introduction

When a passion for travel meets an eye for detail the landscape steps up and delivers. Unlike many photographers, I have seldom waited for an opportunity to capture scenery on film. On the contrary, it appears to find me, something for which I am most grateful. I can happily move through landscapes of immense proportion, knowing inwardly that when the time is right, all the conditions will come together and the moment will be captured.

Landscape photography is very much about this synergy of conditions. Within every photograph lies a compositional complexity, mostly immeasurable, but broadly comprising subject, texture, line, depth and lighting. Personally I do not notice any particular one of these; rather I sense when what I have in front of me will reward me with a photograph of visual value. I have heard it said that the camera is a necessary evil, a tool for the capture of images, but an item of equipment which has no inherent value without the skill of a photographer. People just beginning their journey into photography often confuse the importance of the camera with that of the photograph, and I suspect that some seasoned professionals drift into this thinking also.

Understanding the significance of the final photograph contributes largely to its value as an object of art, a fact which has helped me earn a living from my photography since 1995. In striving for that final photograph, though, endeavour is not everything: my motives, mood and method having some relevance too. In the humble text strewn through this mostly visual book, I strive to take you behind (or more accurately in front of) the scenes so that you may have a glimpse of my world. If I am successful, then the photographs alone will convey character and mood, and a visual journey through this book will provide valuable insight into the dramatic remnant of Gondwanaland that we refer to as Southern Africa.

'I have introduced this collection of photographs almost as though it wouldn't matter where they were taken, but of course it does. The character of each place has an almost mystical ability to be clearly observable in the simplest of compositions'

My reference to our area within the continent of Africa in purely geological or geographical terms is intentional, as man-made boundaries are ambiguous: landscapes transcend boundaries, and boundaries of land-ownership often meander along rivers, themselves exquisite subjects for landscape photographers. Furthermore, the character of the terrain spanning such boundaries may be intensely diverse, or may be almost visually uniform, rendering the boundary meaningless in photographic terms. To me it does not matter. Perhaps my short time as a geologist in the early 1990s has influenced me; at the very least it has accentuated my appreciation for landscapes and provided a depth of understanding of my subject from which we photographers benefit.

Landscapes lie at the heart of many people's lives. They are the core of memories, of what we call home. They can quite literally be the grounding upon which generations grow and nurture their offspring, build their homes and watch each day dawn. Photographs of significant events in people's lives touch their emotions, and yet many of these photographs are not of events alone, but rather of events against a familiar background of mountains, farmland or coast. Heartfelt moments are captured in such photographs, and revisiting any photograph stimulates new moments of pleasure and reveals new detail. This is how landscape finds its broad appeal without the limitation of boundaries defined by politics, culture or circumstance.

I have introduced this collection of photographs almost as though it wouldn't matter where they were taken, but of course it does. The character of each place has an almost mystical ability to be clearly observable in the simplest of compositions. My own favourite places are captured in this book and, since there are so many of them, some of them might be, or become, yours too. The viewer's experience is always a personal one, however, and I wish you any benefit you might derive from them.

10 | Kalahari, Northern Cape, South Africa. Following pages: Western Cape, South Africa

14 | Underberg, KwaZulu-Natal, South Africa

'Landscapes lie at the heart of many people's lives.

They are the core of memories, of what we call home'

Abandoned

'Noticing abandoned items lying on dunes and amongst the grass makes one wonder about the people who have been there before: about their goals and aspirations, and whether they achieved them with any success'

It is perhaps unusual for an opening chapter to convey such a sense of finality, but if we consider the timelessness of our scenery we realise that our impact on it, although significant, is ultimately temporary. Or at least we hope so. Scenes depicting the structural decay of buildings have always fascinated me; the permanence of the landscape is emphasised by its contrast with our fleeting attempts to house ourselves or drive ourselves to work. Having been a geologist makes me uncomfortably aware of how little time humans have spent on Earth ... perhaps we should spend that time more wisely.

I have photographed abandoned items in many locations. Kolmanskop, an old mining town near the bleak coastal edge of the Namib desert, rates highly in my estimation for its strange juxtapositions of sand and brick, sandblasted glass windows and rooms filled with dunes. Sand remains (for me) a key element required for a place to be a ghost town and, although abandoned villages exist throughout the world, I equate 'ghost town' with 'Kolmanskop'. In my many visits there I have experienced it differently, but most memorably when on my own, the solitude of which further enhances the aura of abandonment. Given that I am a bit of a loner by nature, a substantial proportion of my photography has been undertaken alone. I do enjoy a close relationship with my family, however, and some of my best photographs were taken with my three boys playing happily behind me, ever careful not to walk footprints into freshly blown pyramids of dune sand.

Footprints haunt me in my travels. Aware that I leave my own, I am often disappointed by the existence of other people's. The self-centredness of this disappointment is a character trait probably better not explored here, other than to justify it somewhat by saying that my goal in ghost towns is to depict them photographically as if no-one were there ... at all. This leads me to the point that part of the secret of being a landscape photographer is to remove one's own importance from the scene, and to allow the scene to exist for everyone equally. With this aim in mind, I 'abandon' my scenes once I have captured them, wanting to view them as anyone else would.

Noticing abandoned items lying on dunes and amongst the grass makes one wonder about the people who have been there before: about their goals and aspirations, and whether they achieved them with any success. I feel both privileged and cursed to be alive during a time of such rapid change, and I often question if those of preceding generations felt the same way. Most situations can be viewed relatively, meaning that there is no absolute truth in our perception of the world, and with the great choice of pursuits, objects and paths which we have in the twenty-first century, it is up to us to choose wisely and positively. I believe that creating photographic art from the abandoned products of the pursuits of previous generations is one such positive choice.

20 | Kolmanskop, Namibia

Light and dark are significant in photography. Indeed, a traditionally good black and white photograph contains extremes of both; otherwise it melts into a greyness better suited to an image of a wet winter's day in Cape Town, clouds and mist obscuring a glorious view of the mountain, than to a prize image whose splendour will last hundreds of years.

In Kolmanskop these extremes of lighting exist for interior photographs and, moreover, interiors contain dunes normally found outdoors, thus providing an exterior feature lit by interior conditions. To handle this lighting, photographically speaking, I let some of the brightness and darkness disappear into themselves and retain no detail. This is both necessary, since film cannot tolerate such a huge range, and welcome, since it lifts the scene beyond that of a simple documentary.

One of the marvels of living now lies in the advent of digital photography, certainly a worthy replacement for film, but a phenomenon which has done as much to make photography simpler as it has to confuse people about its role. Although digital photography provides considerably more options and manipulative power than film, I enjoy using either and accept either as valuable if the resulting photograph is worthy. All but two of the photographs that appear in this book were taken on film, but I don't profess to be a purist: the photograph is the end which justifies the means.

'Sand remains (for me) a key element required for a place to be a ghost town and, although abandoned villages exist throughout the world, I equate "ghost town" with "Kolmanskop"'

24 | Near Keetmanshoop, Namibia

Near Fish River Canyon, Namibia | 25

'Scenes depicting the structural decay of buildings have always fascinated me; the permanence of the landscape is emphasised by its contrast with our fleeting attempts to house ourselves or drive ourselves to work'

Karasberg, Namibia

Pursuit

'Although I approach most potential photographs visually, I am often motivated by another aspect of the scene'

A visit to Pilgrim's Rest in Mpumalanga could be confused with time travel: part of it feels old, and the other part is a modern exploitation of its history. Walking the streets one feels as if each step is a step backwards or forwards in time. Quaint modern coffee shops, fuel stations, impromptu car washes in parking areas and suitably tarred roads vie with museums and jaded facades for attention. Humans have always pursued what works for them at that time, and so we end up with a rich mixture of past and present in one place. It is very obvious in Pilgrim's Rest, as the town still exists simply for the sake of preserving it. The nearby magnificent Blyde River Canyon, by comparison, exists for its own sake.

The subtle images in the following pages depict South African passions. A nation of avid and talented ball players are reflected in goal posts, often standing in conditions idyllic for visitors but difficult for daily living. The Drakensberg is an area of undeniable grandeur, and home to generations of people who have pursued their daily lives in its rural magnificence, arguably in conditions from which they would have been happy to escape. Although I approach most potential photographs visually, I am often motivated by another aspect of the scene. I try not to question this motive until long after a print has been made, when it lies in front of me ready for inspection. In the case of the goal posts, I found myself envying the people who were able to take the time to indulge in sport with their friends and adversaries, and to enjoy the healthy benefits too.

Choosing a pursuit often casts out the possibility of another, and sometimes we look at others with envy; those pursuing something we ourselves would like to do but through circumstance are unable to. We need to remind ourselves to appreciate what we have.

It might be peace in the aftermath of war (Mozambique, pages 32 and 33), pride in the face of poverty (Mozambique page 38), entrepreneurship within a community (Mozambique page 39) or even simply somewhere to go (Swartberg, South Africa page 36, and Maputo, Mozambique page 37). When we learn this appreciation, music happens in the most remote places within ourselves and our world (top of Sani Pass, Drakensberg page 35).

Some of these pictures are quite different from landscapes. Although I believe in specialisation, I strive to keep my mind open and to remain willing to follow any prompt if it has value. No-one is completely one track, and since photography tends to amalgamate all of one's interests, some artistic deviance is likely, even for a self-proclaimed landscape specialist such as myself.

'Some of these pictures are quite different from landscapes. Although I believe in specialisation, I strive to keep my mind open and to remain willing to follow any prompt if it has value'

Travel can be an all-consuming, breathtakingly exciting ride through life, allowing one to discover and rediscover places and people. To be able to travel willingly as part of a greater purpose (as I would describe photography) is a gift indeed. Although much of my own time is spent happily at home, I have been fortunate to travel more than most. Making the decision to incorporate travel into one's career requires resolve and a view into the future in terms of one's family's needs, for example. Fortunately my family support me and for that I am grateful. They say fortune favours the brave, but I know that doing what I love to do to earn a living is far less brave than spending hours in traffic only to arrive at a job which one cannot imagine enjoying. To people stuck in this position, I would firstly recommend that they find the beauty already around them, and then not fear finding a beautiful pursuit.

Swartberg Pass, Western Cape, South Africa

Maputo, Mozambique | 37

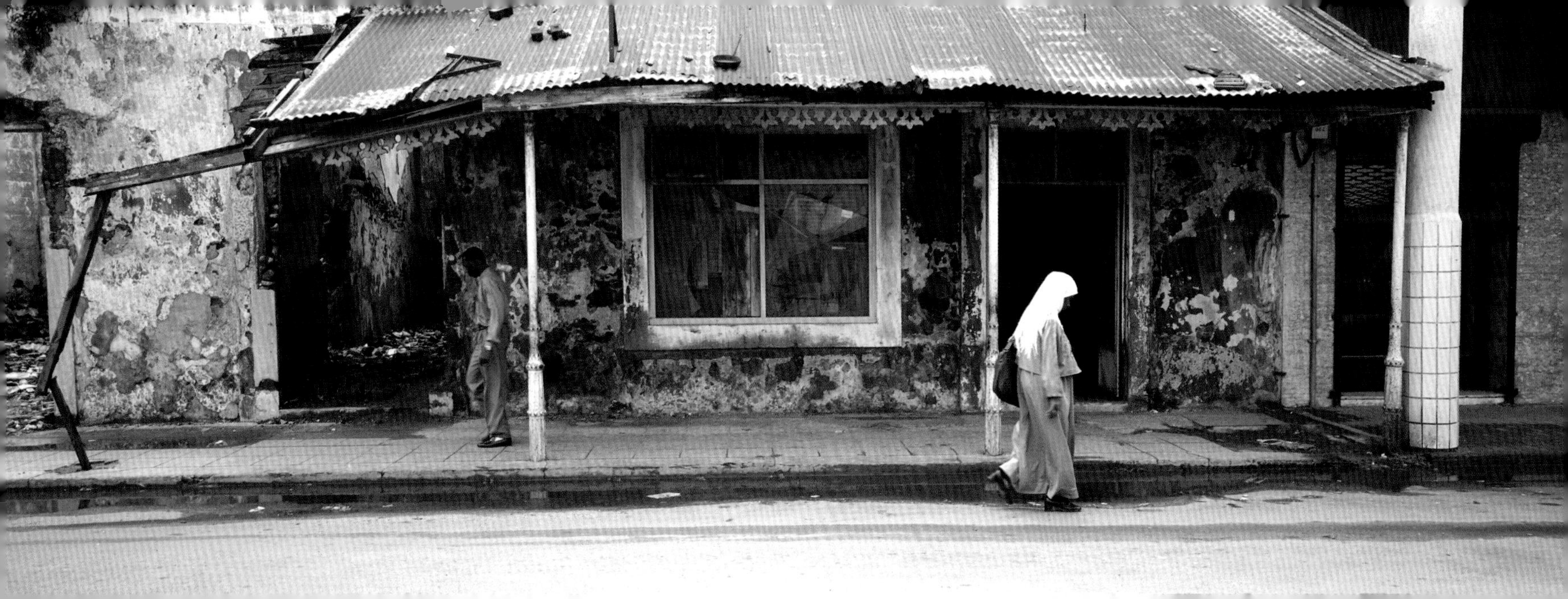

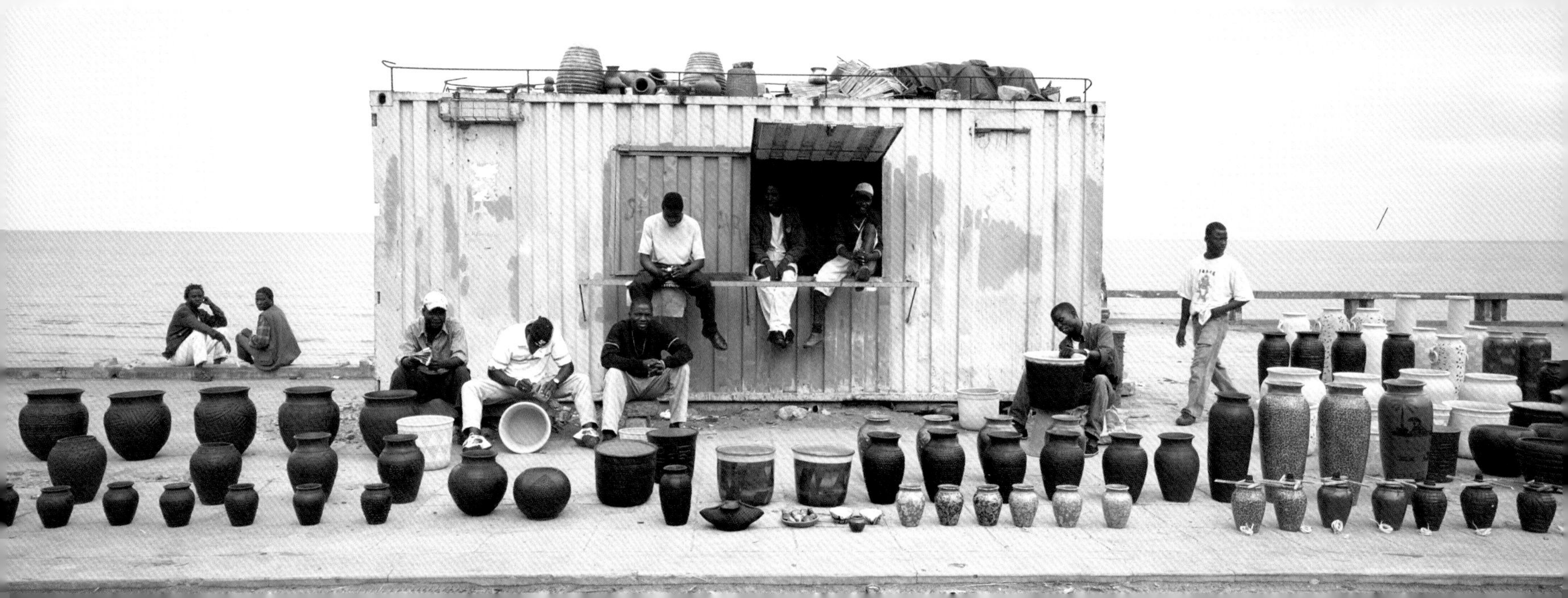

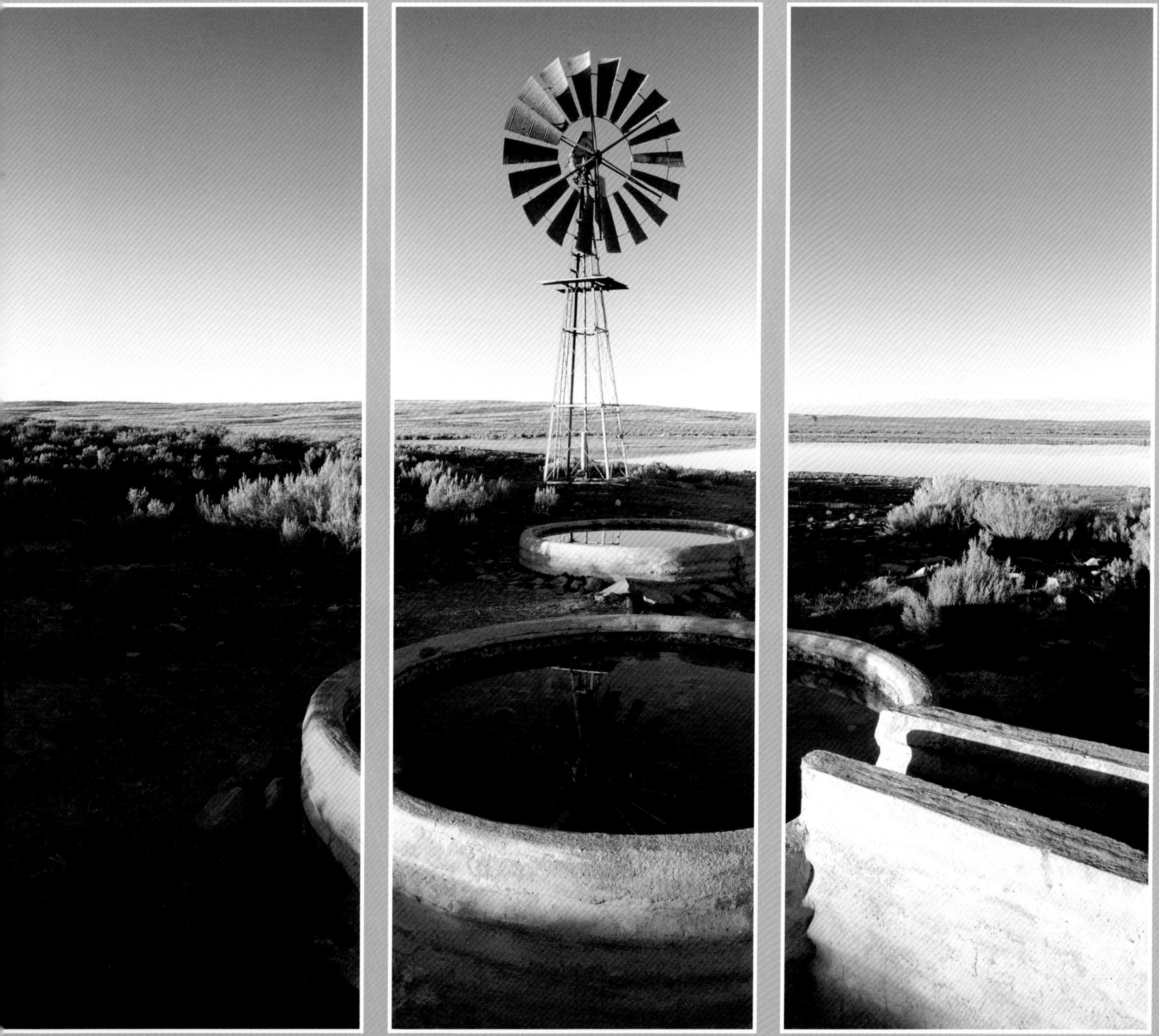

Thirst

Perfection is one of those elusive concepts that can only ever exist in our own minds

    The desert exudes a special silence. It is, in fact, neither quiet nor motionless, and wind can transform the barren landscape within seconds. But it feels silent. During and immediately after wetter summers, fresh shoots of grass completely modify the defining colour of the surface. And yes, in the desert, colour is a major aspect of composition, but one of the many secrets of life is knowing what to leave out. It is not so much that colour itself takes away from line, form and texture, but rather that any extra information might do just that. And so, again like life, compositions should be kept simple. And it is in deserts, particularly the silent Namib, where this is easy to do. On a grand scale these landscapes are as simple as landscapes can be, with usually clear skies, curling dunes or craggy, dry expanses of rocky outcrops. On a medium scale, vegetation grows in splendid isolation, allowing the photographer to choose careful focal points. On close inspection, complexity takes over and the myriad life forms and minute details are awe inspiring, if not entirely photogenic. Within these obvious features lies the real magic, the organic patterns and curves that are as good a representation of perfection as I have ever found.

    Perfection is one of those elusive concepts that can only ever exist in our own minds. Those seeking it often try to locate it in a physical sense, and rather, more importantly, believe that perfection equates with absolute consistency or in things being identical. Blemishes are identifying features and are fundamental to character, and within character lies perfection. No-one looks for a soul mate under the heading 'characterless', and locations would have less impact on our senses if they too were characterless. Within that character most of us also look for some integrity, and for want of a better word, some direction. This is where 'imperfect' shape within the features of the landscape, or even defined by the features of the landscape, can represent the most ideal visual circumstance for a photographer.

Within the Namib so many types of landscapes exist. The pleasure in searching for them lies in moving, particularly in an east-to-west direction, when the vegetation becomes sparser and gives way to exposed surfaces of seemingly infinite textures. Chasms carved out by sporadic fluvial enthusiasm reveal riverbeds lined with fractured and bent geology, overlain by cascaded rockfalls and sediment brought downstream, providing just enough remnant groundwater to sustain substantial communities of twisted and aged trees. From the surrounding plains distant seas of red dune sand lie partly hidden behind protruding rocky hills, left bare by thirst and exposure to fierce extremes of temperature.

Further west, and behind layers of travel, lies a coastline of very limited hospitality but for the wealth of diamonds lying in submerged terraces and in just enough quantities within the sands to have spawned entire towns, like Kolmanskop, now lying in near desolation. Further north than Kolmanskop, beyond the grandness of exceptionally sized dunes and into the bleakness of the Skeleton Coast, lie half-buried, weathered ship hulls washed viciously onto the land during Atlantic storms, storms survived only by huge colonies of seals and tumble-polished pebbles. It is, indeed, a land of dramatic contrast and stark, parched beauty.

43

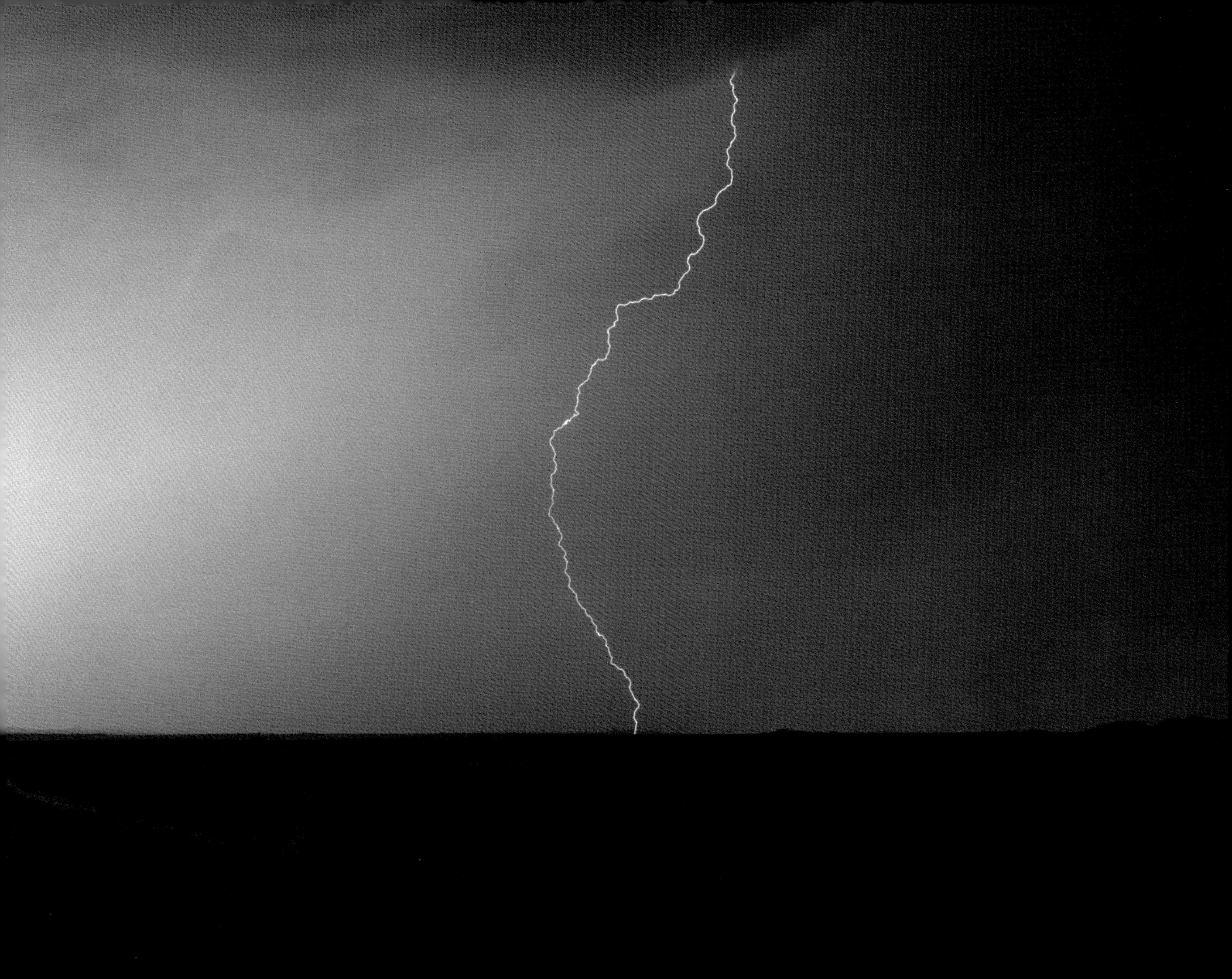

46 | Near Aus, Namibia. Page 47: Southern Cape Coast, South Africa

It would take a lot to convince me that the 19th and early 20th century inhabitants of this area experienced much beauty, even between the sandstorms which kept families indoors and wore down the very structures built to give shelter and provide infrastructure. They must have been hard souls, and indeed mining as a pursuit might be inclined to produce hardness in people drawn into it mostly with the promise of a handsome paycheque.

Luckily for some, paycheques can take on vastly different forms, and I bet that for the very luckiest just being alive is payment enough. I on the other hand need more to experience a worthwhile life, and to earn a bit to pay my way through it, and I am happy not living permanently with candlelit dinners and boarded windows.

Modern evolution has brought with it carbon-fibre tripods, sophisticated equipment backpacks and the ability to store thousands of pictures on a card barely the weight of a large coin, and photographers equipment now weighs very little. But it is in simplicity that we are able to travel light. And, as a general rule, travelling light reduces the inertia that prevents our changing direction in life.

I must admit that I have never climbed to the top of one of Sossusvlei's 300m high dunes. In nearly ten visits I have watched countless people do just that, people who are up for a challenge which I have preferred to find elsewhere. Having been to the top of some other places I can vouch for the view and, having now made my confession, I will undertake to make the most of my next trip to Sossusvlei.

Making the most of anything has always been fundamental to my being, though I do give careful consideration to what 'most' actually is. None of us can achieve everything, and the very fact that I return to the same places many times reminds me that there is no real achievement, only experience, and with that in mind I try to leave something new to do on the next excursion.

Fish River Canyon, Namibia | 49

50 | Sossusvlei, Namibia

'The desert exudes a special silence. It is, in fact, neither quiet nor motionless, and wind can transform the barren landscape within seconds. But it feels silent'

52 | Kolmanskop, Namibia

'Personally, to grow photographically I immerse myself in my subject and I let that do the teaching'

54 | Kolmanskop, Namibia

I have at times given photographic direction to amateur photographers looking to improve their skills, train their eye or gain some inspiration. Of course, being amateur has no bearing on ability, but making photography one's profession sends out a resounding message, and often a decision of this magnitude is the most fundamental part of a process of change. In much the same way, the decision to abandon the town of Kolmanskop must have been one made with awareness of its impact on the people who grew up there and carved out a settled existence within the solid wood doors and décor-rich walls. With any big decision one needs the perseverance to change completely. My ability to provide guidance is ultimately limited to the example I have set, and my words might not be nearly as inspirational as a visit to the interior of present-day Kolmanskop. Personally, to grow photographically I immerse myself in my subject and I let that do the teaching.

56 | Southern Namibia. Page 57: Sossusvlei, Namibia

Every few years the desert at Sossusvlei comes alive with the ingress of water from the Tsauchab River. The water from rains further east flows ferociously across the desert, channels through the Sesriem Canyon and plucks rounded boulders from the canyon's walls, finally coming to rest, not in the sea surprisingly, but on an impermeable clay pan surrounded by dunes. The tumbling pebbles never make it this far; the water alone with its consignment of suspended clay settles peacefully into its new environment. Gemsbok drink amongst bright green plants for months afterwards, until the strengthening summer sun burns off the remaining moisture, leaving only a mosaic of thick, concave slabs of white clay. These crumble to softened mudcracks, determined to outlive the dryness and once again experience the flood. Dead sculptured trees keep lookout. Water is life in the desert, and through natural circumstances nature's dam provides a cycle of disappearing oases to challenge the very existence of flora and fauna.

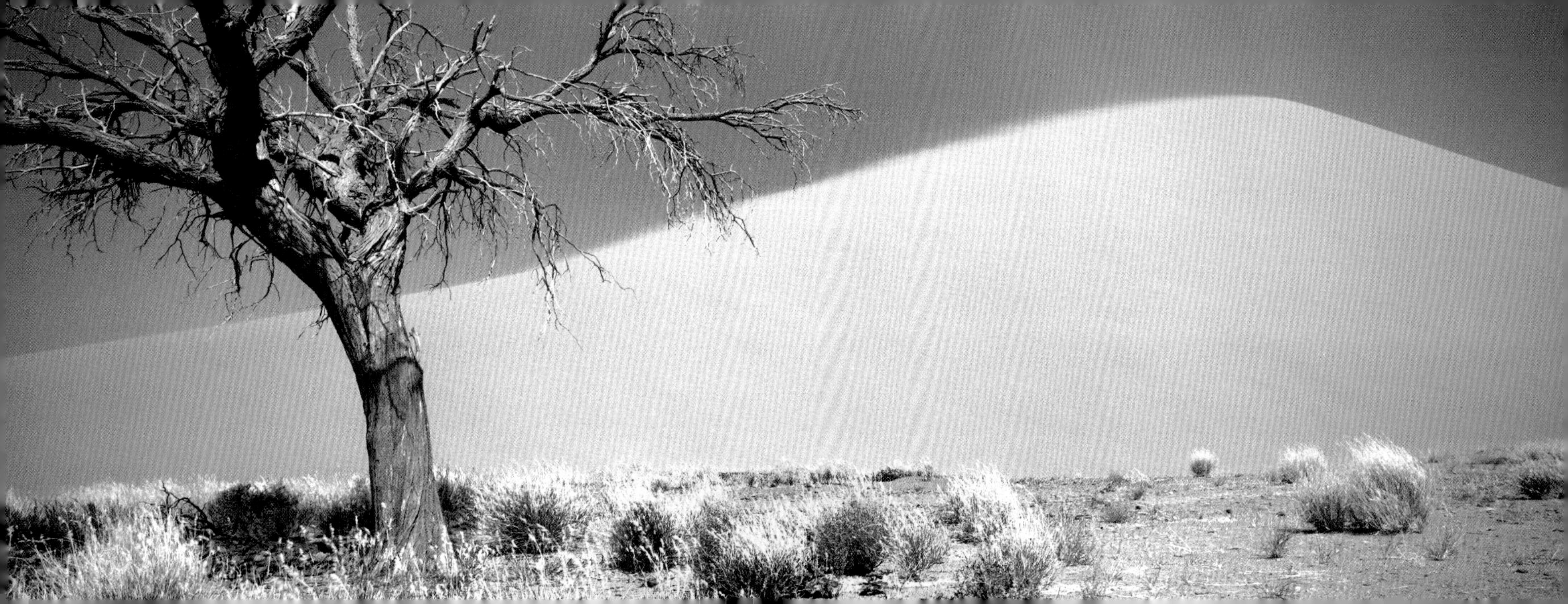

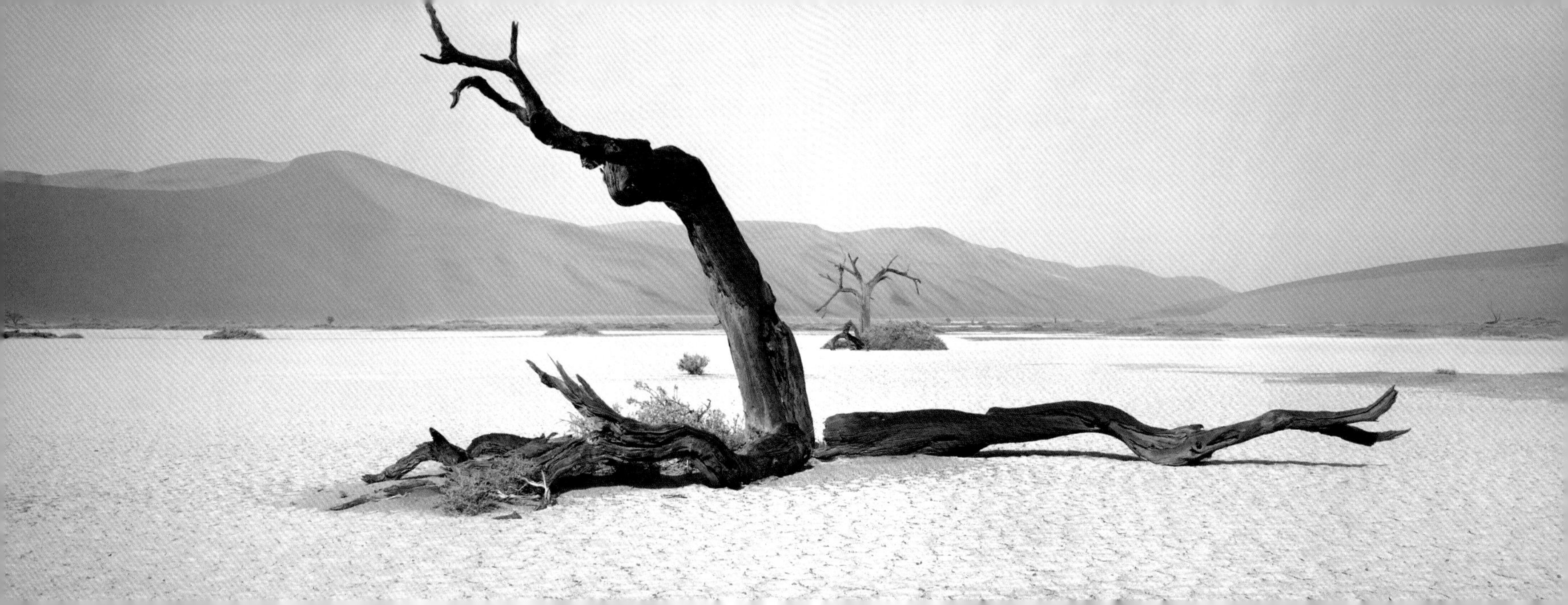

Sossusvlei, Namibia

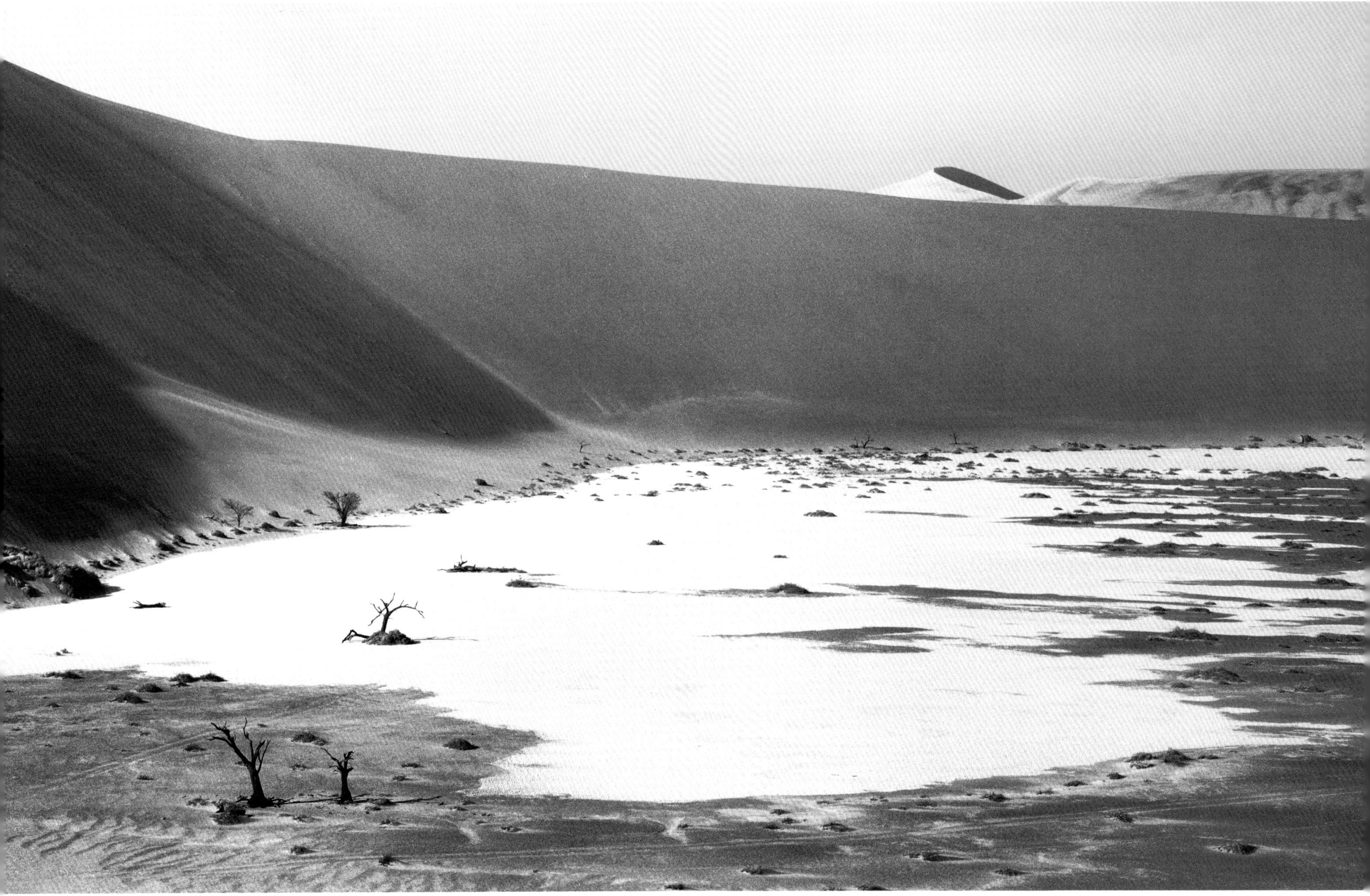

'As a general rule, travelling light reduces the inertia that prevents our changing direction in life'

On the way to Maltahöhe, Namibia | 63

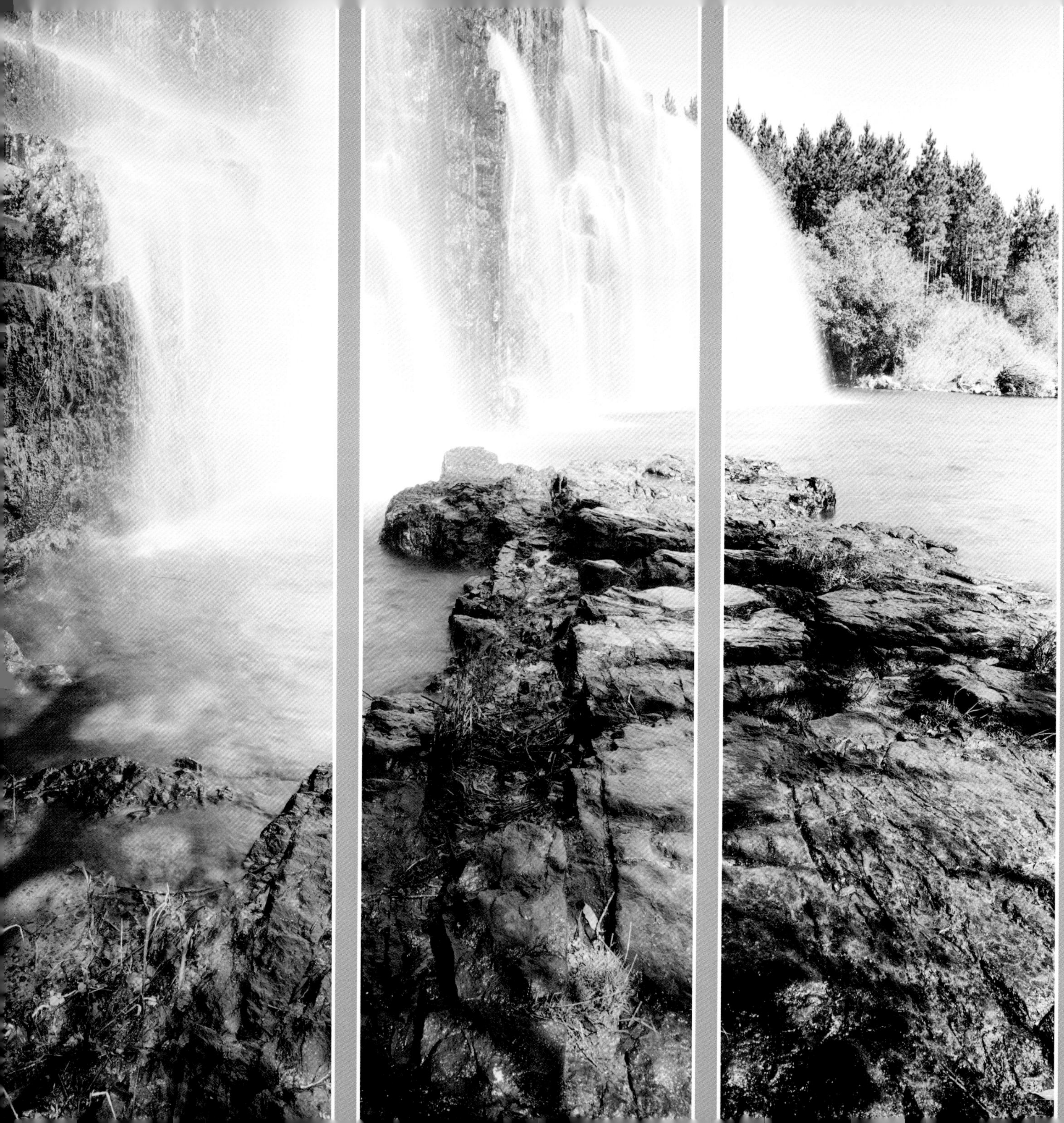

Water

'The water cycle is a dynamic one, and Southern Africa is an interesting locale for its study'

The practice of photographing water is apparently known as 'hydrosculpture'. A shutter opening of significant duration is selected on the camera, and water, moving as it does because of wind or gravity, is rendered blurred on the film or CCD. Since the surrounding terrain remains stationary, rocks, trees and buildings render sharply in the final picture. During this exposure of the film the camera must itself remain stationary for any chance of success. It is a very easy process, and the resulting textural contrast produces a mood of pleasing tranquillity. By means of pictures borne of technical manipulation, it is evident that this is just what water does. It flows seamlessly downhill, contrasting almost effortlessly with the channel in which it flows. The seeming effortlessness belies, however, the fact that over time significant removal of hard material occurs. The water cycle is a dynamic one, and Southern Africa is an interesting locale for its study.

The east and the west are separated cartographically by a line known as the 500mm Isohyet. This is a line joining places of equal annual rainfall, in this case 500mm, and the theoretical boundary between arid and arable. The escarpment edge known as the Drakensberg forms an orographic barrier to warm Indian Ocean air, and thunderstorms are regularly unleashed amongst the cliffs and peaks during summer afternoons. This, along with seasonally widespread rain and a generally humid atmosphere, produces a multitude of rivers which empty into the Indian Ocean after carving a steep journey across the province of KwaZulu-Natal. On the western side of these mountains, the deeply carved hills of Lesotho give way to an immense geological area known as the Karoo, where flat-lying sedimentary rocks have produced a largely flat and mostly waterless region.

66 | Seymour, Eastern Cape, South Africa

Although seasonally arid, the Karoo is farmed extensively in many areas, and low density livestock can be seen grazing in the sparse shadows of rocky mesas. These table-top mountains are capped with the remnant rock of a younger layer, carved away mostly by the action of water in the millions of years since it first formed within a vast inland, slightly bowl-shaped, sea. The evolution of this sea was related to decreasing water: the earliest material was deposited underwater, the more recent material was blown in by an arid wind. Glacial deposits were also part of the very complex sequence of events which helped provide a canvas for landscape photography. The pictures I take capture moments somewhere in a continuum, in an ongoing process. And water is one of a few very powerful, tireless elements at work.

Further northwest from the Karoo lies a semi-desert: it is wild and grassy, with a burnt-orange carpet of yellow grasses and brick red sands offset by a deep blue sky. The contrast can be impressive in black and white too, and the region's character, as always, shines through. Water is more of an event than a sculptor here, summer rain soaks away quickly into porous soils, feeding dormant seeds.

Storage of water and the ability to direct natural water into these vessels of storage are vital in the drier regions of Southern Africa. Ubiquitous farm dams are scattered everywhere, in various stages of fullness. I remember from my days of science that dams are the structures holding back water, and reservoirs the water itself. Either way, both make good subjects. Even more iconic within our landscape are the windpumps, rattling and squeaking in the breeze, extracting water from the ground and filling overflowing cement dams. Photographs of windpumps could fill a book on their own, but in this one they feature sporadically, not least on the cover.

Apart from differences in clarity, colour or content there really is not much to distinguish one body of water from the next. Once a river merges with the sea, for example, it releases its load of sediment and becomes one with the ocean. Philosophers argue that the ocean simultaneously becomes one with the river. Obviously a straight cut through water is difficult to achieve, and we conclude that water is therefore inseparable. I think this conclusion is valuable and that this can be taken further: as the photographer of a scene, I too merge with the scene in front of me for a moment. It fascinates me that, as with water, we are all, after all, just atoms. More practically and photographically speaking, I would say that a reflection in the surface of water is as real a feature as the water itself.

Page 68: Kunene River, Angolan/Namibian border. This page: Sutherland, Karoo, Western Cape, South Africa | 69

Blyde River, Mpumalanga, South Africa

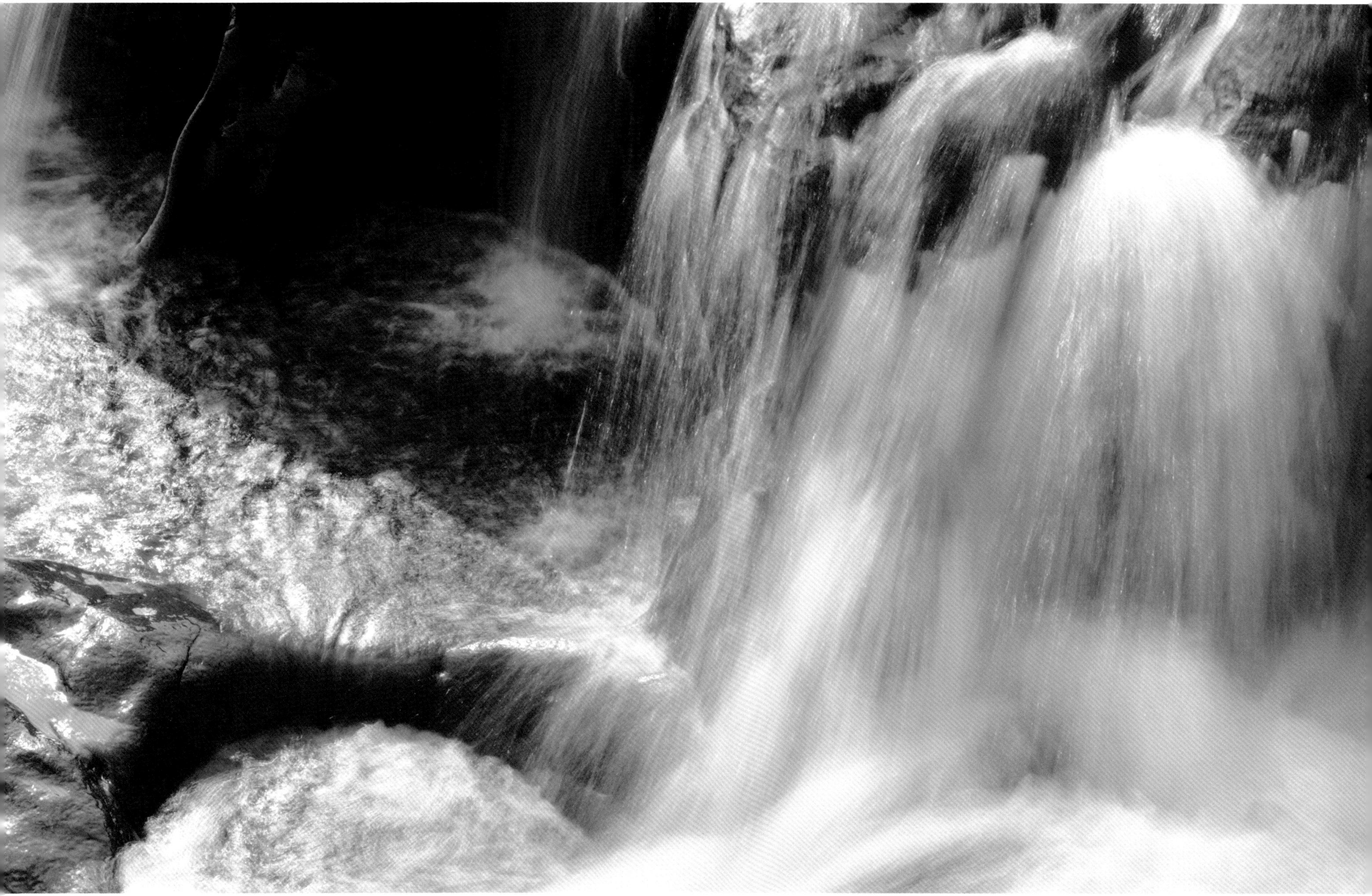

72 | uThukela Gorge, KwaZulu-Natal, South Africa

If you were to sit down and read this text from cover to cover, largely ignoring the photographs in between, you would discover a distinct overlap across the various themes. It is impossible to consider desert and not discuss water, for example. My own philosophies are much like this also; they cannot exist in isolation. This is the basis for synergy, and the Earth is our most successful example thereof. Water above all other possible themes has relationships with every other theme; we are made of it, it is in the air, the ground and the chemicals I use to process my photographs. The massive abundance of water in the oceans that continuously moves between the poles and sweeps around continents continues to shape the surface of our planet. It is through an intense thirst for both water and experience that I am driven to walk kilometres to find a waterfall or to wade deeply in the embrace of a powerful river.

'...this is just what water does. It flows seamlessly downhill, contrasting almost effortlessly with the channel in which it flows. The seeming effortlessness belies, however, the fact that over time significant removal of hard material occurs'

Blyde River, Mpumalanga, South Africa | 75

iDidima Gorge, KwaZulu-Natal, South Africa

77

Growth

'I am very careful not to alter my scenes at all before taking pictures. I try not to move branches or trample plants even by accident ...'

During the first part of this study of Southern Africa, and buried within the text, which I hope provides only a helping hand to the photographs, character has had some significant mention. I learnt during my time in a photographic club that many critics are inclined to evaluate the success of a photograph by identifying all the individual elements that make up a composition. It is, however, the character or presence of a photograph which contribute to its success, and this is a product of every aspect combined. I try not to think of each aspect; instead I compose my photographs by instinct and intuition, and if I have any awareness of line, texture, focal points or lighting, then this is with me so briefly that it might as well be instantaneous. We identify character in our scenery in a similar way. We just know it when we see it, and it is the thing we miss most about home when we travel far away for too long.

A surprisingly big component making up character is vegetation. Maybe this is not so surprising, when one considers that vegetation relates so distinctly to the underlying soils, weather patterns and the like. Some trees and bushes seem to grow anywhere, but others such as the Eucalyptus tree from Australia do not in fact feature strongly in some places: Namibia, for example. Thus vegetation defies the tendency to uniformity so characteristic of globalisation. Actively removing alien trees and bushes provides a more original environment in which indigenous plants can thrive. I applaud these efforts, although the spread on page 98 now looks rather different without the trees. It is also now the site of a complex of townhouses, and ultimately nature has not been restored.

Thankfully the photograph remains, and we must not forget that, photography is a very effective means of recording how things are at any particular time. Times change, trees are cut and new ones seed themselves into existence elsewhere.

Hex River Valley, Western Cape, South Africa

Perhaps my only reservation regarding the advent of digital photography is its potential for metaphorically blurring reality. But then manipulation of photographs is seeded in ideas, and ideas are every bit as real to the owner as trees are to the soil in which they grow.

    I am very careful not to alter my scenes at all before taking pictures. I try not to move branches or trample plants even by accident, perhaps out of a sense of treading lightly on the world in general. I find that the more I connect with nature through my photography, the more careful and aware I become, and the more I grow spiritually. I would love to live in a world where grass does not have to be cut, where nature does not have to be disturbed, and where I could have a positive impact. I admire, for instance, those people dedicated to preserving areas of natural bush I so love to photograph: the Knysna forests, the windblown coastal forests of KwaZula-Natal, and the mangroves, fynbos and quivertrees found in various places in Southern Africa. An incomplete list, certainly. The various national and regional authorities set up to oversee this preservation do a fine job indeed, and I am glad to be part of the process by drawing some attention to the beauty of the region.

80 | Fish River Canyon, Namibia

Aloes, Kareedouw, Eastern Cape, South Africa | 81

The tenaciousness of many trees reminds me of some people I know. I admire the character of those who fight for their survival in all its forms. When undermined by forces beyond our control it is easy to back down and collapse into some safer place. We can run and hide, unlike the tree which remains statically balanced and vulnerable. No matter what our chosen path, there are times when we shy away from our perceived threats, often doubting our intentions and accomplishments. In the world of art this is no different. Good times bring a sense of manic joy, but these are transient. It has taken me too long to be able to view myself from further away so that I may exist comfortably in the knowledge that trusting my path brings the reward I require. And I believe we get what we require, not necessarily that which we would like or ask for.

Page 84: Costa Do Sul, Mozambique. This page: Keetmanshoop, Namibia | 83

'The tenaciousness of many trees reminds me of some people I know. I admire the character of those who fight for their survival in all its forms'

This page: Garas, Namibia. Following pages: Swartberg, Western Cape, South Africa | 85

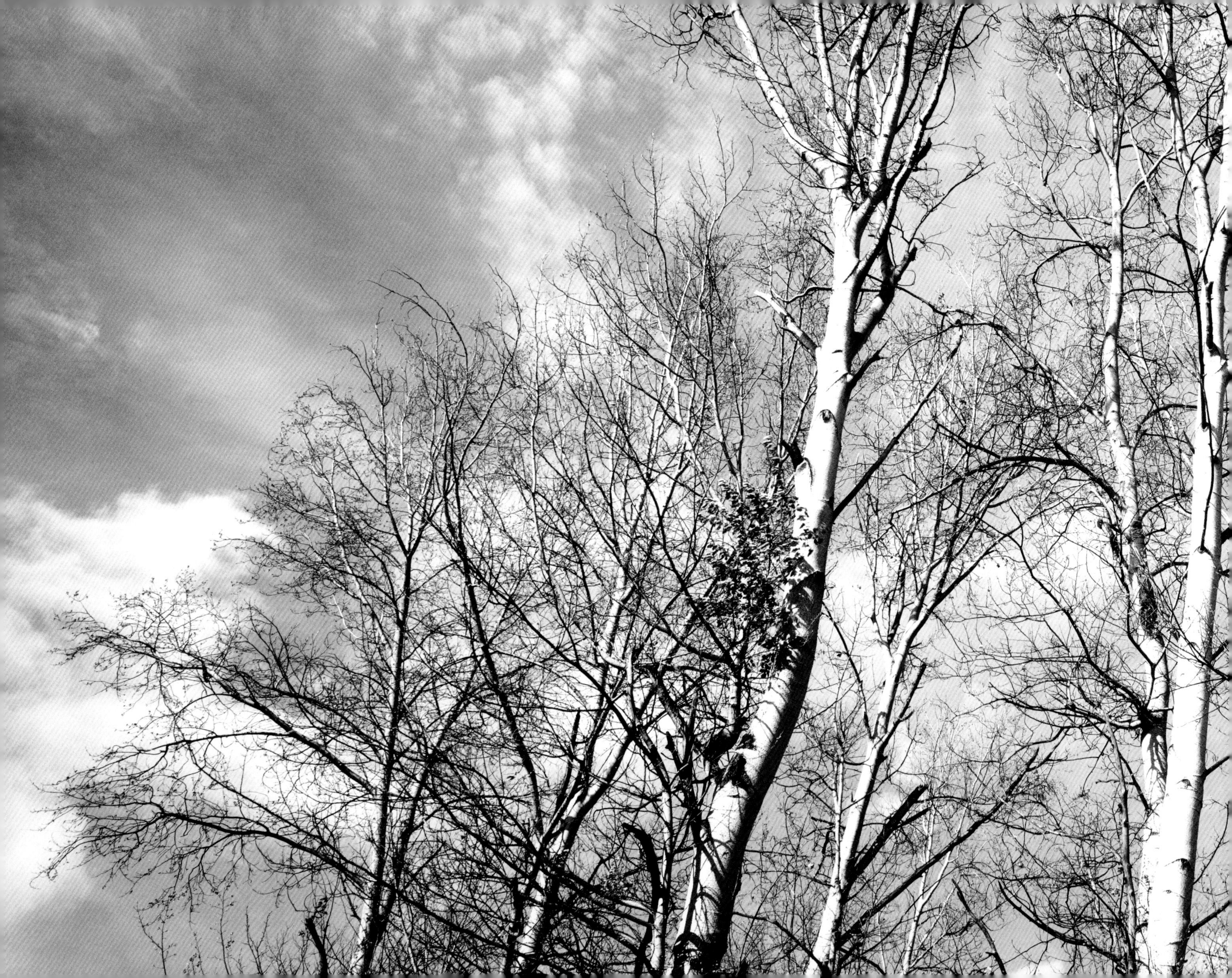

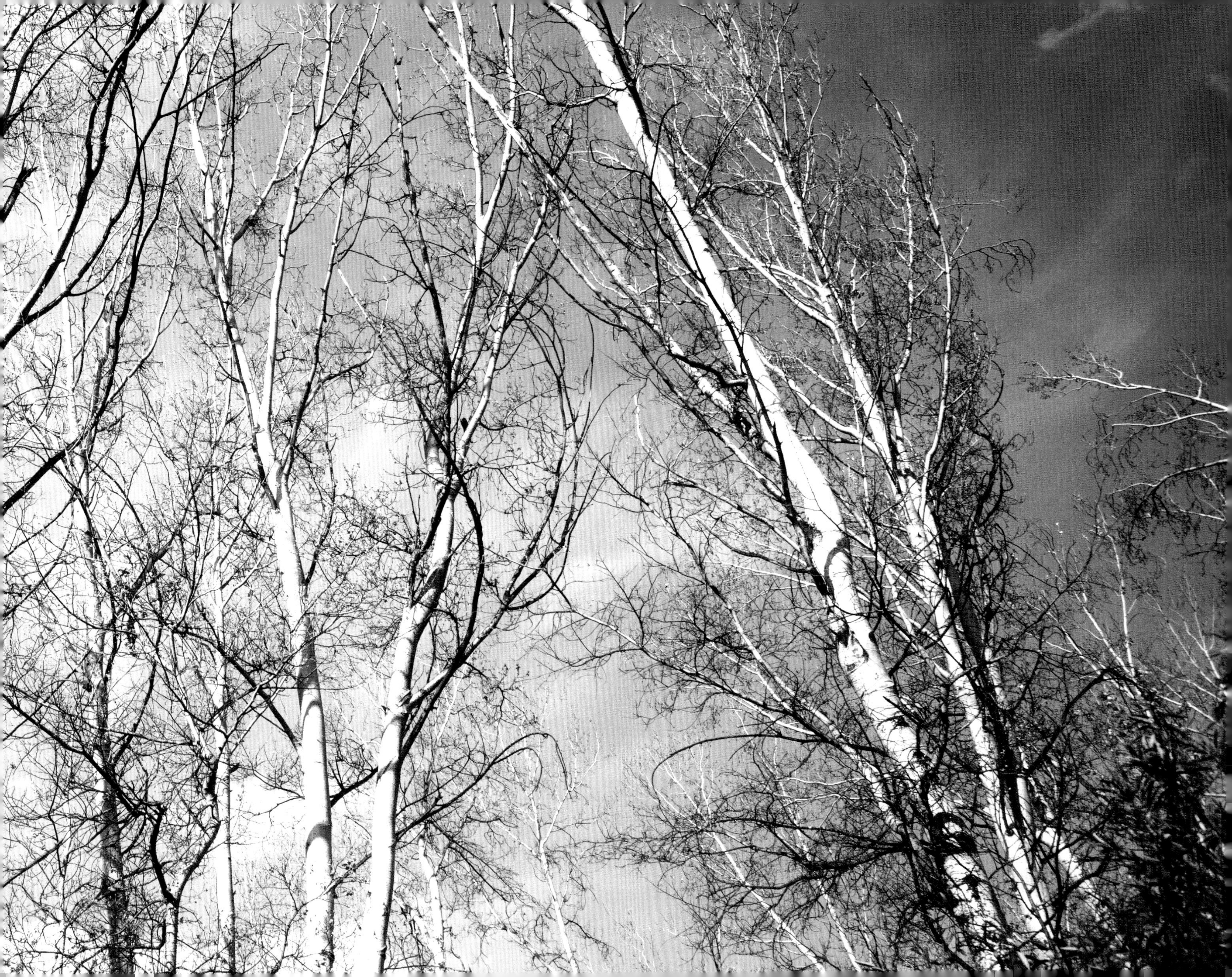

Between Rosh Pinah and Aus, Namibia

Of all the indigenous plants, the quivertree is probably my favourite. It is a sculptural masterpiece which also happens to grow in some of my favourite parts of the world too, across a region extending from the Northern Cape through to south central Namibia. They create wonderful silhouettes, both to the naked eye and to film. They are rather intriguingly named quivertrees because the bushmen used their hollowed-out stems to make carriers for their arrows; to me they look like quivers already full of arrows. Quivertrees characteristically enjoy feeding off dolerite rock outcrops, and dark, iron-rich boulders can therefore often be seen strewn around the base of thinly arranged forests of these 'kings' of the aloes.

Growing up in KwaZulu-Natal, I spent many very pleasant family holidays in the Drakensberg mountains, and later took epic hikes and experienced some of the coldest nights humanly possible in a tent in Southern Africa. The impression these trips left in my memories have shaped and modified my outlook, and left me with a continual yearning for the outdoors, although not specifically for the Drakensberg; I have felt at home in many natural settings in various parts of the world, and I am indebted to my parents for instilling in me this enjoyment of the outdoors from an early age. My own children have had the same benefit, and how they will grow to maturity knowing their countryside so intimately is something I will watch with typical parental fascination. My preparation for many of my photographs has involved making sure that my children are safely playing at least a few metres away from my tripod.

KwaZulu-Natal Drakensberg, South Africa | 91

iNjisuthi, KwaZulu-Natal Drakensberg, South Africa

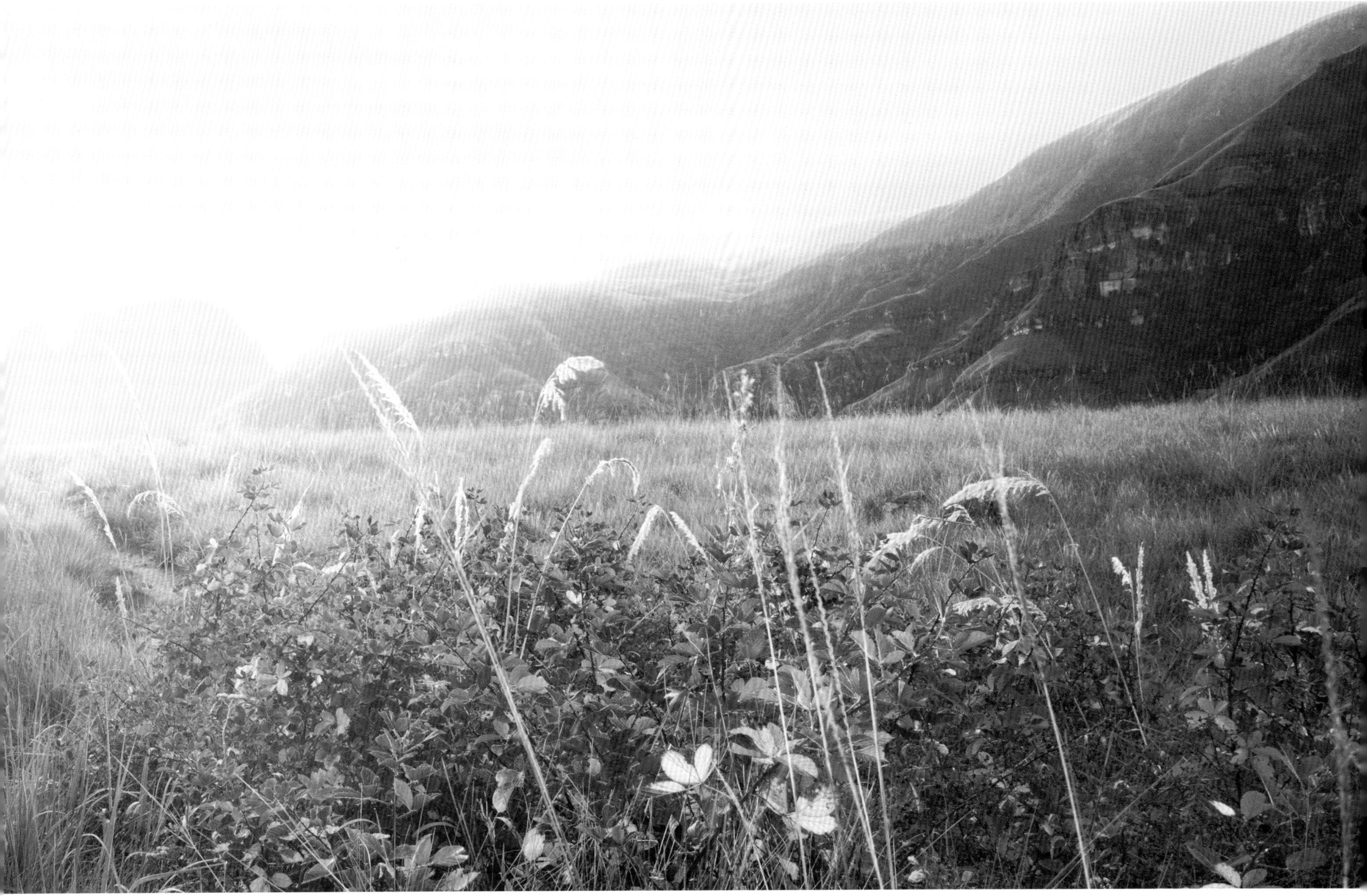

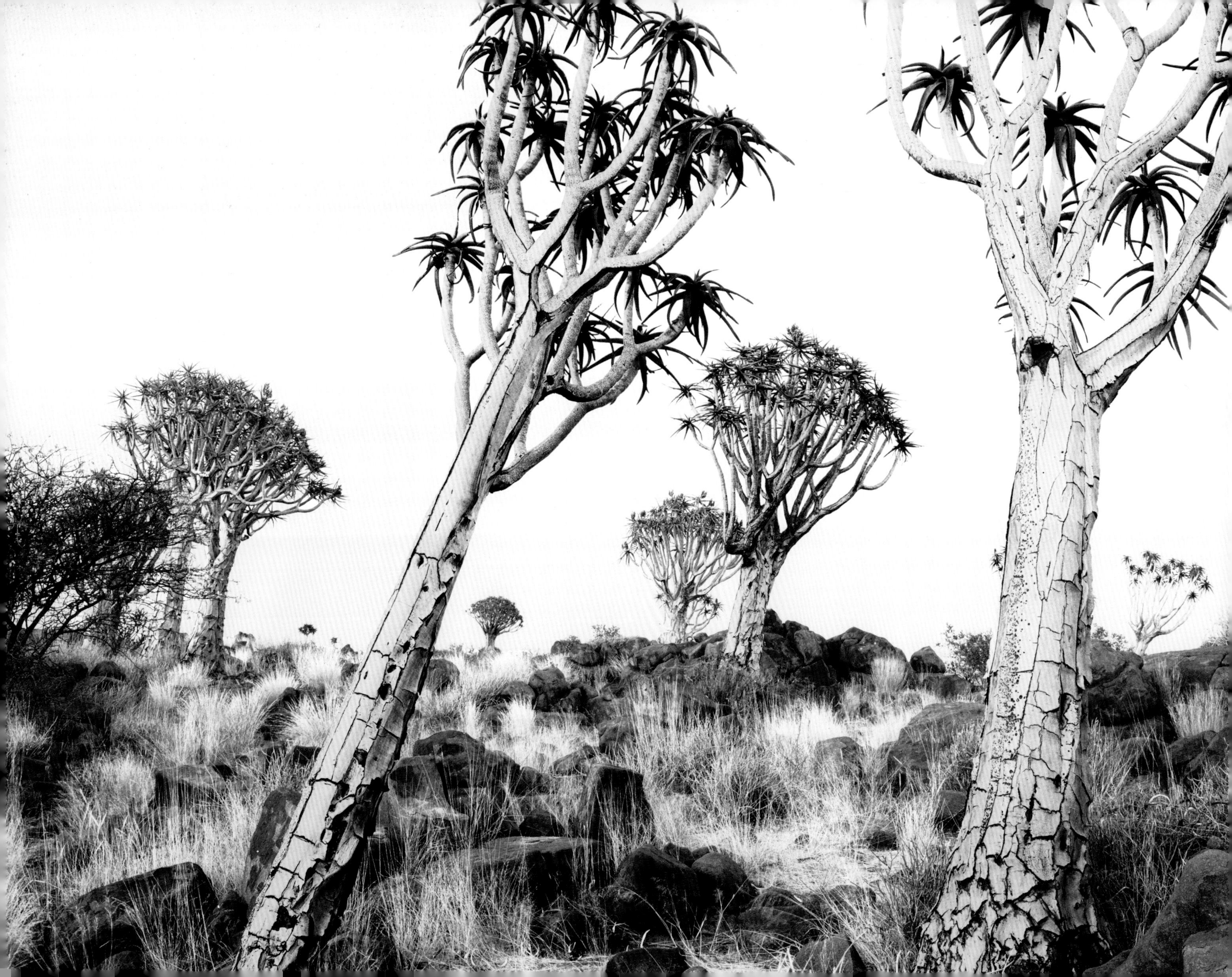

'Of all the indigenous plants, the quivertree is probably my favourite. It is a sculptural masterpiece ... They create wonderful silhouettes, both to the naked eye and to film. They are rather intriguingly named quivertrees because the bushmen used their hollowed-out stems to make carriers for their arrows ...'

Keetmanshoop, Namibia

Knysna Forest, Western Cape, South Africa

Mozambique/Swaziland border | 97

98 | Gillitts, KwaZulu-Natal, South Africa

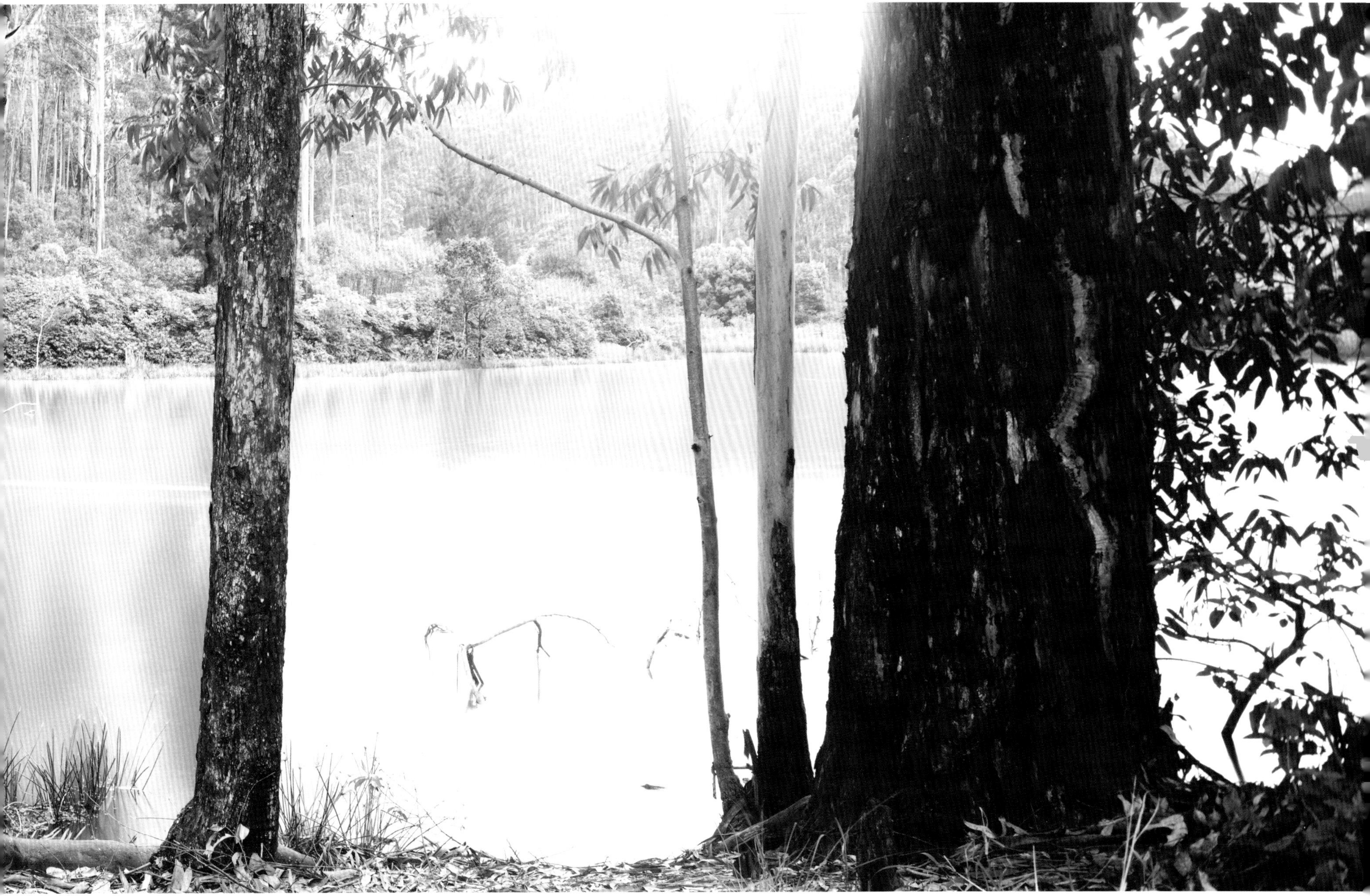

Knysna, Western Cape, South Africa

Himeville, KwaZulu-Natal, South Africa | 101

Limit

'Where deserts are largely peaceful and quiet, the coast provides a more dynamic relationship between visitor and seascape, with its crashing waves, the salt-filled air and the abrasive nature of the coarse granite sand'

Sea level is used as a significant reference point in most descriptions of a geographical nature: above it, below it, away from it and how much it will rise if the gradual warming of our earth forces the annual temperatures of the polar regions above that of an average winter morning in the Karoo ... The sea has been a more general point of reference for me too, having lived my formative years within walking distance of the Indian Ocean. During my early adulthood I frequently immersed myself in it, and between the looming, rideable sets of waves, the waiting became a meditation and an exercise in patience, from which I continue to benefit. I remember reading many scientific papers in our university library, straining to see the quality of the distant surf between piers which reached out into the sea beyond the white foam. Southern Africa has a wealth of beaches, from windswept west coast beaches to rocky coves, to world-renowned surf breaks. The weather in the region is equally idyllic, and provides a multitude of different reasons to visit the lagoons, the expanses of white sand and soft dunes. For photographers the pleasures are obvious; we find subjects in abundance with relative ease.

Where deserts are largely peaceful and quiet, the coast provides a more dynamic relationship between visitor and seascape, with its crashing waves, the salt-filled air and the abrasive nature of the coarse granite sand. The rhythmic sound of erosion is ever-present, softened to background by our mind's ability to adapt. This adaptation is both a blessing and a curse. In the modern era we are fed an impressive array of information, and within this sensory bombardment some very real inspiration exists. I think we miss a lot of it, mostly through this ability of our mind to use adaptation to simplify the content it has to process. If we kept the stimulation simple to start with, we might notice messages of real value much more readily.

A challenge on our coastline, and in fact in many of our photogenic areas, is to retain simplicity within the photographs we take to ensure that our photographs communicate distinguishable messages. The viewer shouldn't feel the need to have to study the work in order to gain anything from it. In other words, we must differentiate the photograph from the original view. Documentary photographs generally say 'This is what you will see if you visit the area and stand in the obvious place'. Art photography says 'This is what the photographer saw when he or she became intimately involved in the subject and would like you to benefit visually from this effort'. And since art has more depth than that, it further says 'And perhaps you too will begin to notice the value in making such observations for yourself and to benefit even without a photograph existing'.

This sums up one aspect of art. When art becomes commercially successful, that is acceptable. When a commercial venture tries to be art, it fails. It might look like art, be sold as art, purchased as art and enjoyed like art, only it fails because its motive for existing was to sell, not to communicate, and that includes communication that only existed between the artist and his or her subject. It has value, yes, but with an emptiness that is often tangible and disappointing. A similar emptiness is felt by those of us who are inclined to exaggerate our experiences, or who choose experiences based on what we think will impress others. Such behaviour represents the widespread first-world problem of materialism and an immeasurable tendency to try and compare ourselves with others, and to forget about our own paths through life. Photography, like being in a place of beauty anywhere on our diverse coast, is an expressly personal experience, and this can unlock our ability to experience fulfilment by finding that unique route.

The sea does what it wants. Combined with sand and hydraulic force it wears away the coastline, sometimes with huge force during storms, and always with continual erosive power that softens and rounds coastal features. This natural destruction can form huge arches of rock, where small islands slowly become tunnelled out by the concentrated action of abrasion, eventually breaking through to reveal the sunrise to a fresh piece of beach. This natural bridge becomes ever wider, and the laws of equilibrium dictate that at some point the middle collapses, leaving behind two side-by-side, free-standing features known as stacks. The stresses are continuous, but the consequences are obvious only with the influence of time. Interestingly, many people collapse in a similar fashion when they too experience constant stresses, so the law applies not only to the sea. Luckily, being near the sea is a tremendous release of stress for many people, and I have discovered that photographs of the sea act in the same way.

Keurboomstrand, Western Cape, South Africa

Thompson's Bay, KwaZulu-Natal, South Africa | 105

106 | Buffalo Bay, Western Cape, South Africa

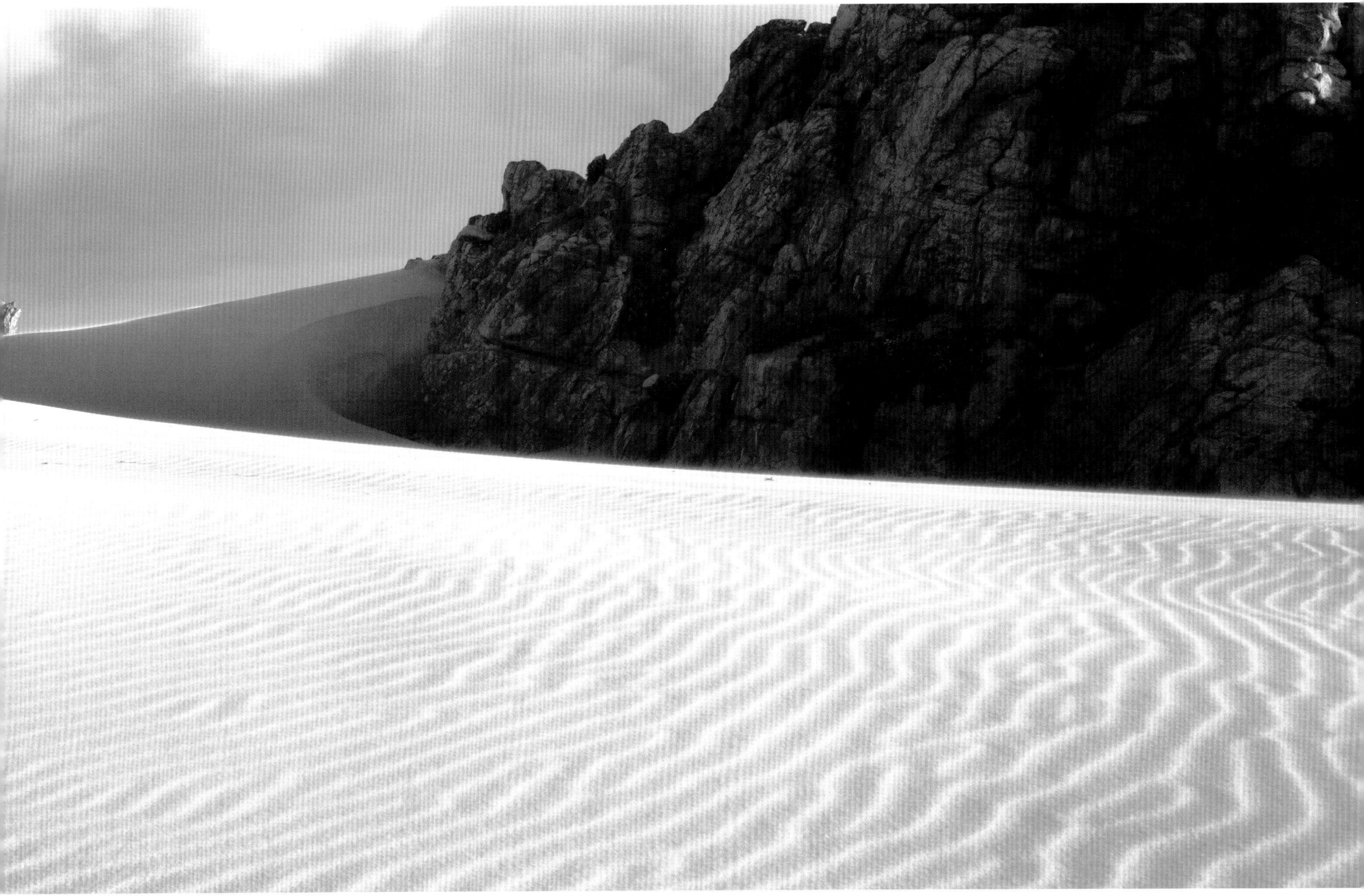

'A challenge on our coastline, and in fact in many of our photogenic areas, is to retain simplicity within the photographs we take ...'

Costa Do Sol, Mozambique | 109

Second Beach, Port St Johns, Eastern Cape, South Africa

112 | Maputo, Mozambique

The sea is a great provider. In the tidal flats of Mozambique, people spend the low tide hours meandering between temporarily stranded boats finding whatever they can to supplement their hunger, and satisfying their entrepreneurial spirit. In Mozambique I ate the best fish ever, and I will retain a lasting memory of its culinary pleasure, as shortly after that I chose vegetarianism in my own attempt at treading lightly in this world. Although personal changes are best made decisively and with conviction, some decisions are much easier to make than others and change is not nearly as necessary where life is simple and peaceful to start off with. In Mozambique people in their communities interact with their environment in the most basic and beautiful ways. Despite the country's rough and tragic past and its ongoing problems of poverty, it appears on the surface at least to have transcended a great deal into a mood of peace.

114 | Durban, KwaZulu-Natal, South Africa. Following pages: Wild Coast, Eastern Cape, South Africa

'The sea has been a more general point of reference for me too, having lived my formative years within walking distance of the Indian Ocean.'

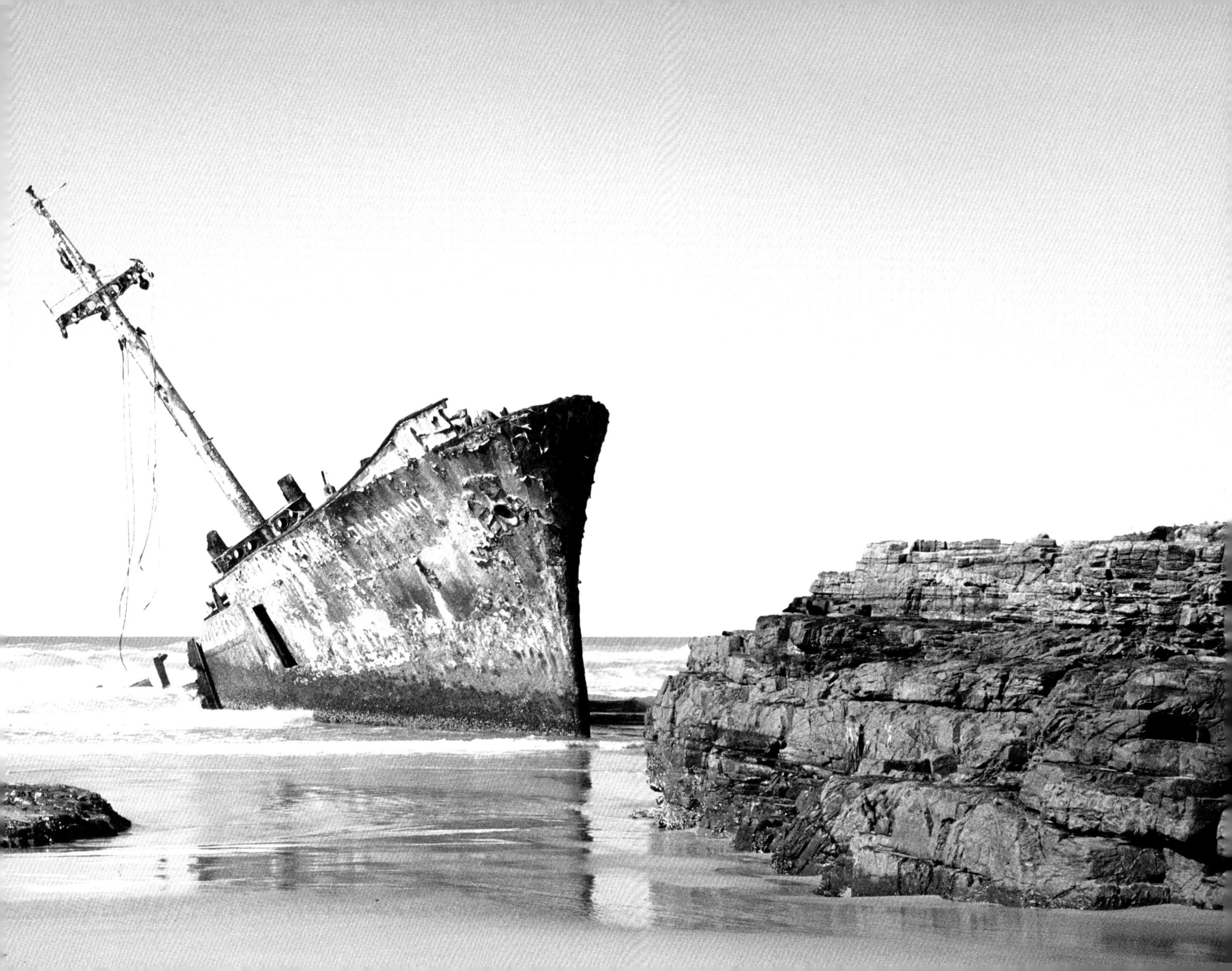
JACARANDA

118 | Umhlanga, KwaZulu-Natal, South Africa, page 119: West Coast, South Africa

Floating on water is very therapeutic. Craft that are not mechanically powered apply very little impact to the water. To leave behind only a wake, and no other record of one's passing by, is fascinatingly similar to taking a photograph. In this respect it is an ultimate form of intellectual property, with no necessary physical expression, but infinite potential value. Boats are thus a win-win blend of peoples' conquest and their ability to preserve the environment. Like all tools, however, they are best used with good care and conscience. I will endeavour to use my camera likewise. In order to do so, I need some grounding of technical expertise, and this can be learned fairly easily from books, magazines and the internet. A course in photography, often inspirational, can teach the necessary skills. It is the greater learning, the rapport with one's subject, the ability to see in a unique and meaningful way, and ultimately to learn about oneself that requires long-term action not unlike the persistence of the sea and its influence on the coast.

Shelly Beach, KwaZulu-Natal South Coast, South Africa

Sheffield Beach, KwaZulu-Natal North Coast, South Africa

uMzumbe, KwaZulu-Natal South Coast, South Africa

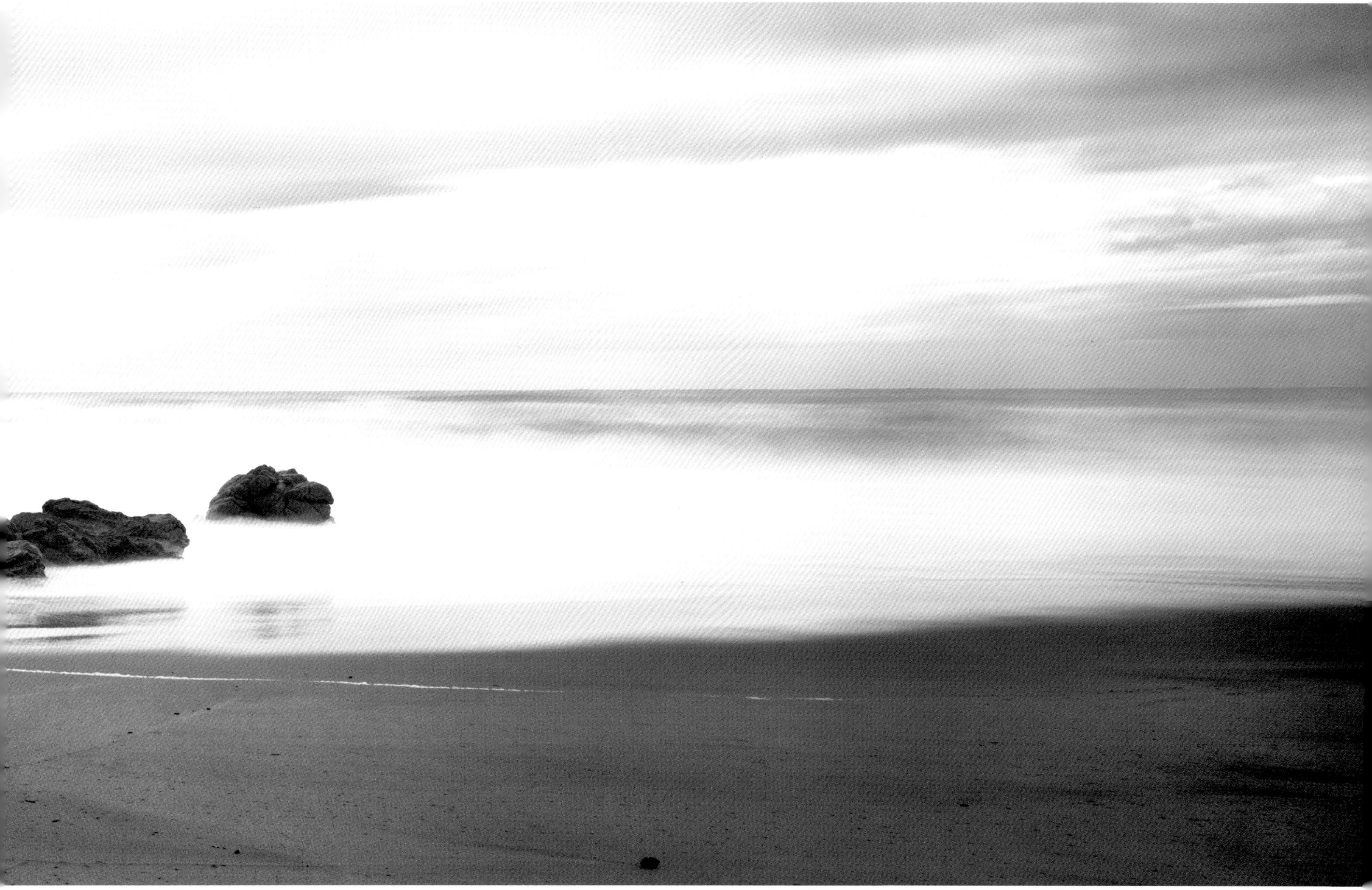

The coastline looks very different from the air. This is of course true of all landscapes. I have had the privilege of flying in various aircraft, and have landed everywhere from runways that appear between washing-line-decorated high rise buildings in Asia to landing strips covered in cows on the Wild Coast, closer to home. Although the start and end of a flight are by far the most eventful parts of any flight and fraught with risk, it is at high altitude that the world becomes two-dimensional and made up of interactions of only line and shape. Although I can gaze for hours out of an aeroplane window trying to spot recognisable places and features, I have always preferred to photograph on the ground, where perspective is available to me and allows me to impart a three-dimensionality to my photographs.

Mossel Bay, Western Cape, South Africa

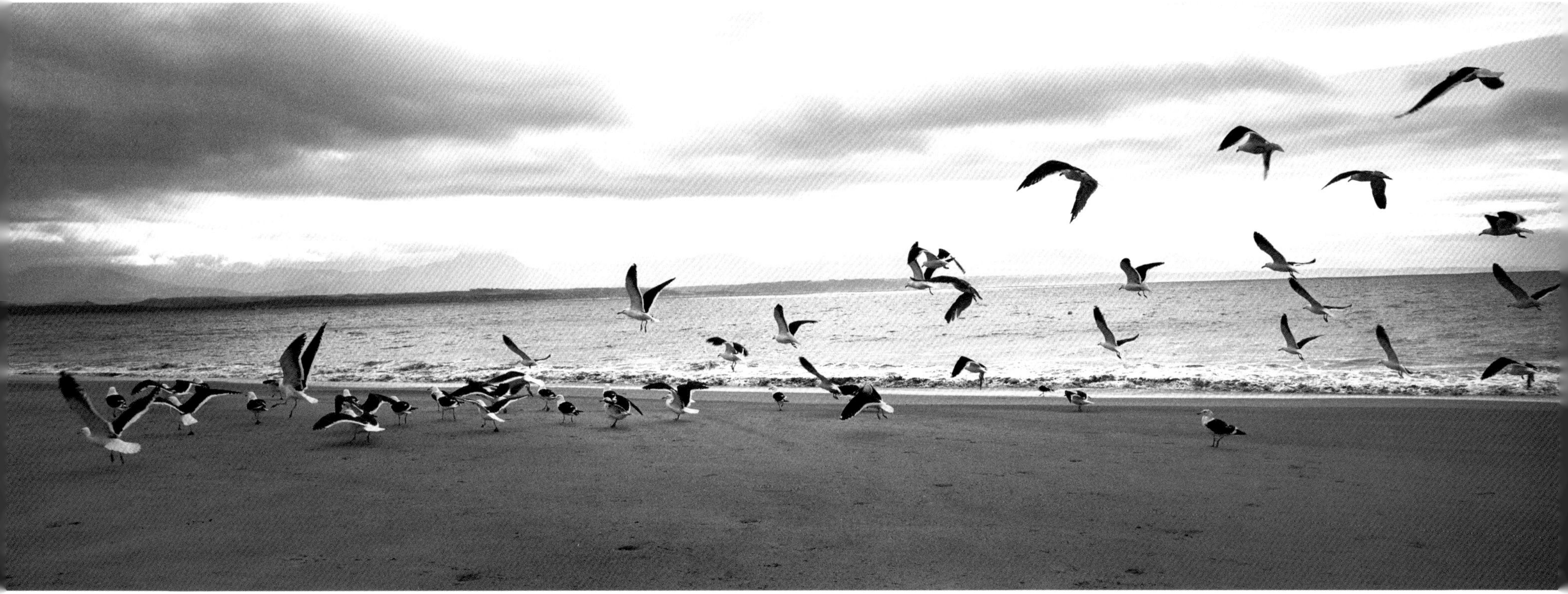

Cannon Rocks, Eastern Cape, South Africa

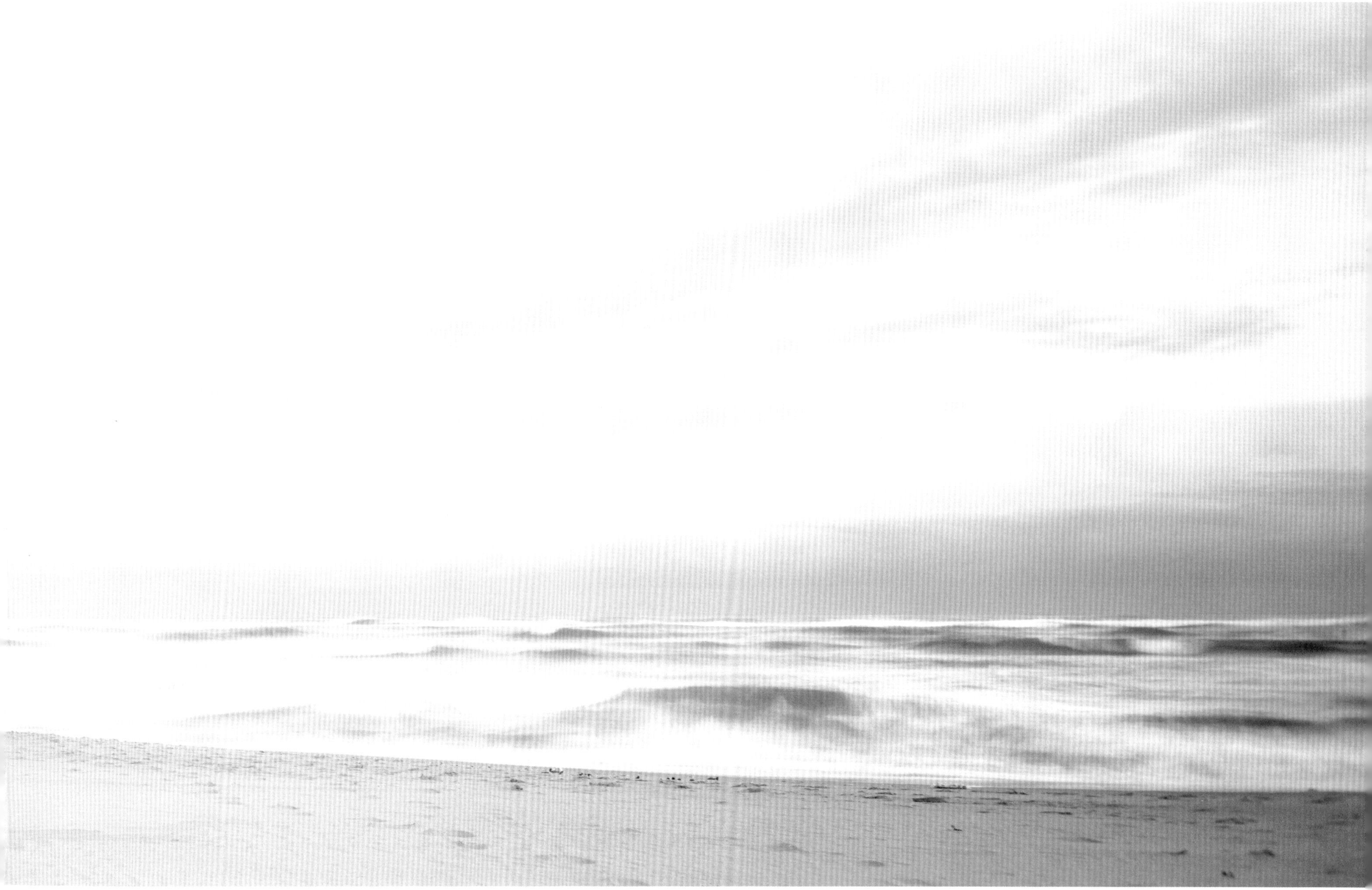

Summit

'Mountains represent challenge to the human spirit, and are in plentiful supply. They provide extreme temperature change, experience gale force winds but offer only sporadic shelter. They trap rainfall and guide it downwards, culminating in cascading waterfalls'

Southern Africa has a geological history which incorporates massive crustal pressure, meteorite impacts, huge basin-filling outpourings of lava, vertical compaction and drying out of inconceivably thick sediments of sand, mud and clay. All of this activity is enough to shape our world into a multitude of peaks and troughs, and almost impenetrable walls of sheer freefall.

Mountains represent challenge to the human spirit, and are in plentiful supply. They provide extreme temperature change, experience gale force winds but offer only sporadic shelter. They trap rainfall and guide it downwards, culminating in cascading waterfalls. Frozen rockpools remind us of how far south in Africa we really are. Huge overhanging caves challenged by gravity frame valleys full of boulders which have long since rolled to a stop along riverbanks.

Table Mountain is our Eiffel Tower, our Statue of Liberty, our Mount Fuji. A close iconic second is the Amphitheatre in the Drakensberg, on the border between the landlocked Kingdom of Lesotho and the South African province of KwaZulu-Natal. A third choice is wide open, but I would add Spitzkop, a giant, Matterhorn-like granite dome in central Namibia. A less obvious Spitzkop, an almost equally Matterhorn-like remnant Karoo peak, exists on a farm by the same name, a farm which I visited with a view to buying 700 dry hectares of it. I still have not made my purchase, but this and other mountains stand, undaunted by their change of ownership for all to admire: Matroosberg looms over the Hex River valley, visible from well over one hundred kilometres away on the edge of the superb Roggeveld escarpment with its highest point, Sneeukrans, my offer on which was rejected by the farmer concerned. Our own history shapes that which is meaningful to us, and in my case it would be unfair and incomplete not to say that mountains everywhere have made themselves felt in my heart: Aoraki, Ngauruhoe and Taranaki in

New Zealand, Kosciuszko in Australia, Mulange in Malawi, Stawamus Chief and Mount Garibaldi near Vancouver, and many others. I nearly ended my love affair with mountains by not ducking when I jumped out of a helicopter on the slopes of Lantau Peak in Hong Kong. Fortunately the rotor missed my head, but the expression on the face of the other alighting passenger who dived on top of me was memorable. I was young at the time, and I now feel more gratitude towards him when I look at my own children.

Photographs of our own families are immeasurably more important on a personal level than any art-motivated photograph of a mountain or otherwise. Sometimes we include ourselves in landscapes, thereby adding personal value to the image. Any reluctance I have in doing this stems from my fascination with time, and how well features such as mountains are representations of timelessness. Having said that, I should mention that Aoraki instantly shrank by ten metres when ice fell from it in the early 1990s, and in more explosive ways many volcanoes worldwide have grown, shrunk or at least caused the surrounding area to re-evaluate the benefits of living with a photogenic view of a cone-shaped summit.

Amphitheatre, KwaZulu-Natal Drakensberg, South Africa

130 | Underberg, KwaZulu-Natal, South Africa

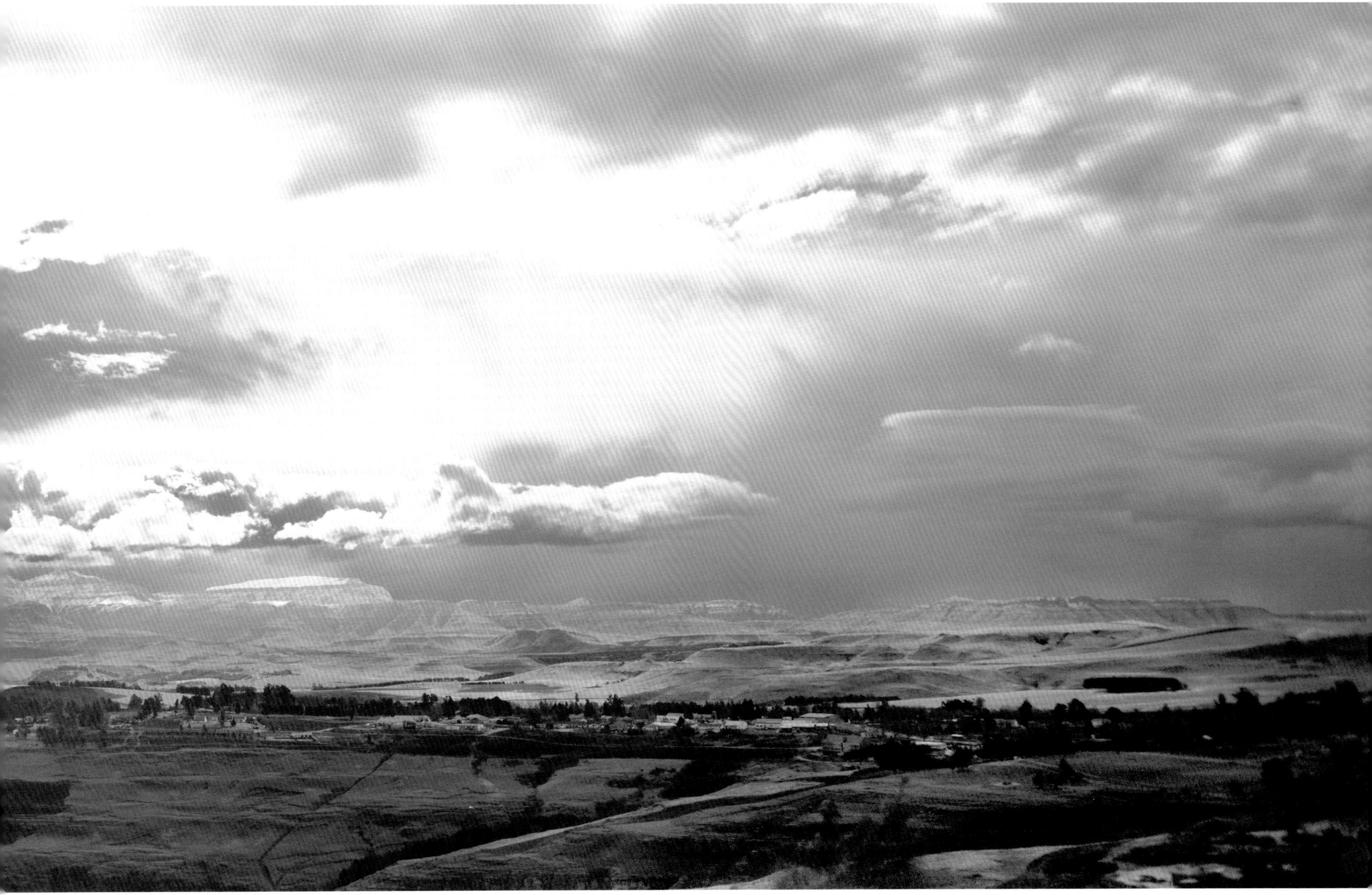

Photographs are like windows. They work in both directions, too; they show us views we may not have seen ourselves, and show us things about ourselves we have never seen. Analysing why we photograph certain subjects is a healthy exercise in self-discovery. And similarly, why we might wish to summit mountains may reveal both positive and negative trends in our psyches. To succeed in life we are required both to strive for success and to relinquish control of the outcome, and this duality invades many of our pursuits and passions. Summits represent the highest point, an ultimate place to be and to readdress goals and values. Too often our goals change, and the things that were important to us no longer have the same value. Paradoxically we battle to experience such shifts in thinking without first having set our minds on a specific outcome or belief. And so I set goals for myself, and then I see what happens during the chase.

Table Mountain, Western Cape, South Africa | 133

Hlalanathi, KwaZulu-Natal Drakensberg, South Africa

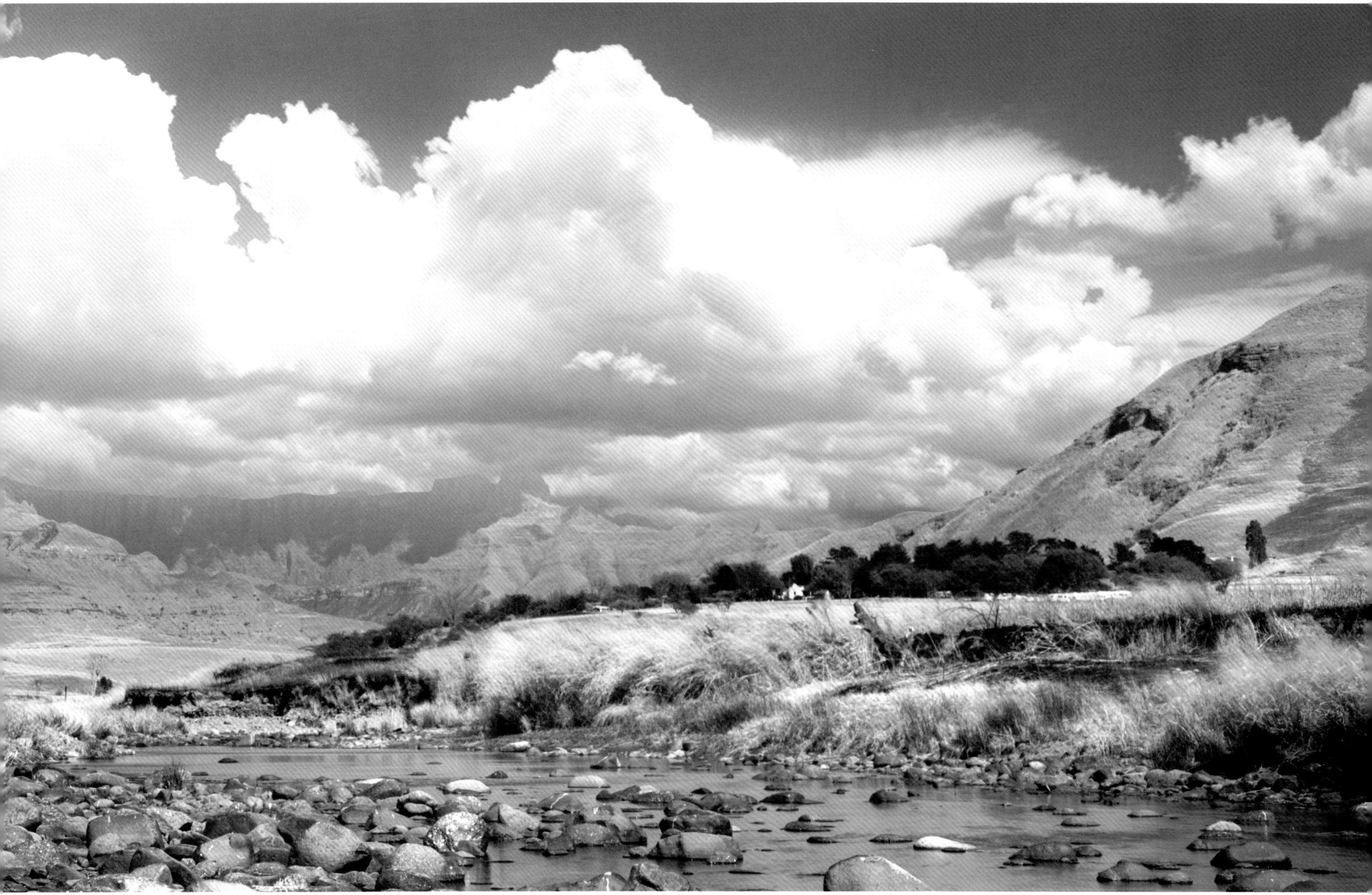

Summits see the day before anywhere else. From such a high vantage point one can look over the horizon and experience the first warming red rays of light. The cold observer in the foothills looks up and sees a mountain basked in 'Alpenglow', a term for the excessively pink-red glow of sunlight striking through a portion of atmosphere so deep that its colour is notably warmer, or redder, than we perceive it to be at mere ground level, even at sunrise. Early in the morning, before sunrise, we can often make out a distinct blue band across the horizon, overlain by a graded pink layer. The blue is our own earth's shadow on the atmosphere, and any mountain poking above that is having sunrise, and if we lived on its summit we would have longer days. Our own outlook is thus relative, and we would be wise to remember that before we judge the quality of the view through someone else's eyes.

Cathkin Peak, KwaZulu-Natal Drakensberg, South Africa | 137

'Photographs are like windows. They work in both directions, too; they show us views we may not have seen ourselves, and show us things about ourselves we have never seen'

Cobham, KwaZulu-Natal Drakensberg, South Africa | 139

Nurture

'Our children are our most important canvasses; they themselves take our nurturing of them and amplify it many times into future generations'

When we are young we are easily influenced. As we mature we begin to choose our influences. As we grow older we realise our influence on others. Since this is a pattern by which we evolve, we must, like the farmer, plan ahead carefully to reap the benefits. We must also find our way in life as early as possible so as to be an example for those still travelling to market. The farmer is a provider, in that his or her benefit is primarily for others, for their sustenance, for their clothing and for their shelter. The benefit of financial gain for the farmer is a fair return for his or her ability to stick with the plan and see the crop through to harvest. Our own influence over others can be potentially positive, inspirational and loving, and so we must work hard to cultivate these character traits in ourselves. To be a healthy influence one must have something to give, and having something to give is the best indicator of having enough oneself. And what better way to be rewarded for one's effort than seeing the best in everything, feeling inspired and being filled with love. And so, our hard toil in the fields of our souls provides us with nourishment.

Our children are our most important canvasses; they themselves take our nurturing of them and amplify it many times into future generations. Having children might not only be completely natural, but necessary for our own growth as people. Teachers must certainly know more than their students, and our children do not have to be biologically ours to be willing learners. On the other hand, the biological bond is a strong protector, but does not seem to prevent some parents from presenting terrible role models to their offspring. Some adults are children, and many children are old souls worth listening to before their ideas and ideals become squashed by a sadly misguided influence.

Where exactly photography fits into this community model has been touched upon during the text in this book, and becomes more clear when we realise that by being forced to observe, choose and communicate as we do with a landscape photograph, we are nurturing a sense of purity, wonder and contribution in ourselves.

Quite apart from the lifestyle that I enjoy through photography, I am able to savour the fact that every photograph is in itself a significant event, and it is the only event that exists for me at any one time. Indeed, any photograph may be the last event I ever experience, and so, as with everything in life I try to appreciate each image in its entirety for what it can provide. I am lucky to have many of these moments, but none is particularly more or less significant than sweeping the driveway, pouring a drink for a friend or building puzzles with a child. In all of these tasks lies value, and each of them can be carried out with love, awareness and appreciation. We may not be granted another chance.

The photograph requires nurturing also. There is a saying that it requires both a lifetime and 1/1000th of a second to take a photograph. This certainly is the case. It takes a substantial amount of time and experience, exactly the age you are now, to see the world in the way you do, so your own photograph has some significant history to it. The act of capturing it is misleadingly quick and easy, as is pouring that drink for someone, but never forget that how you feel and act during this task has been created in you from a long time ago, and yet the choice to live with that awareness is yours to make. I can only hope that my own photographs provide viewers with their own experience, from which they can carry something forward with them, which they can nurture and use positively in our world.

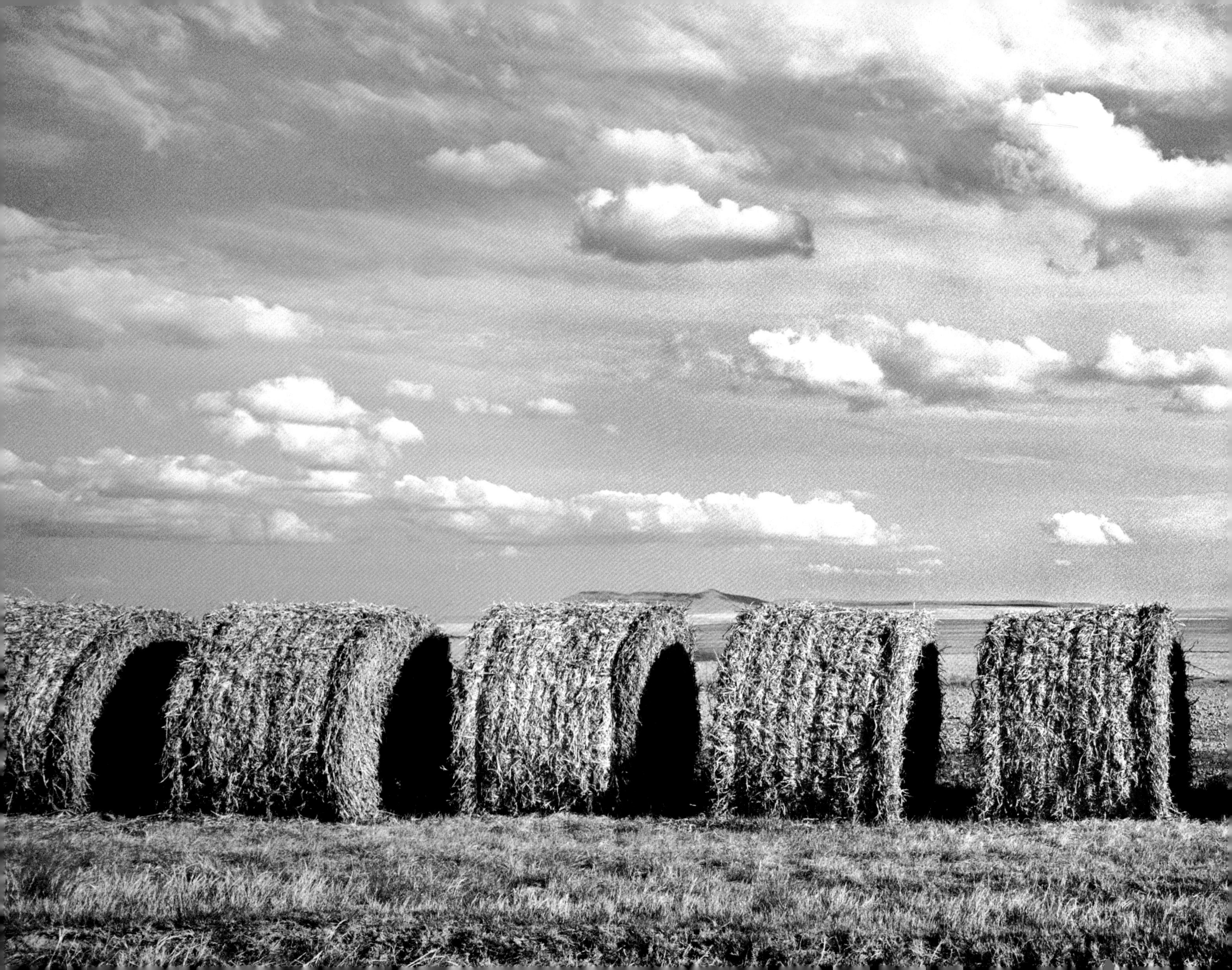

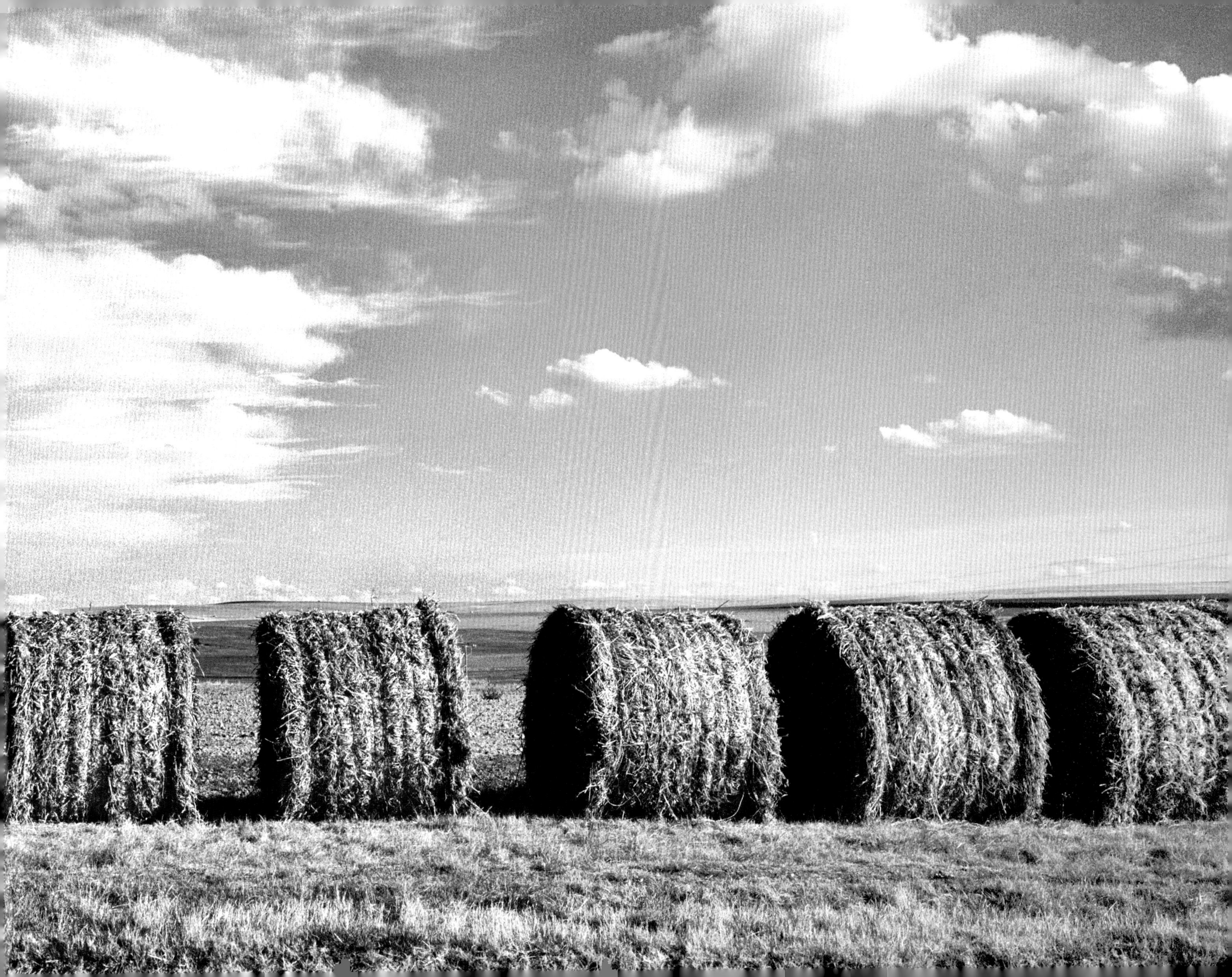

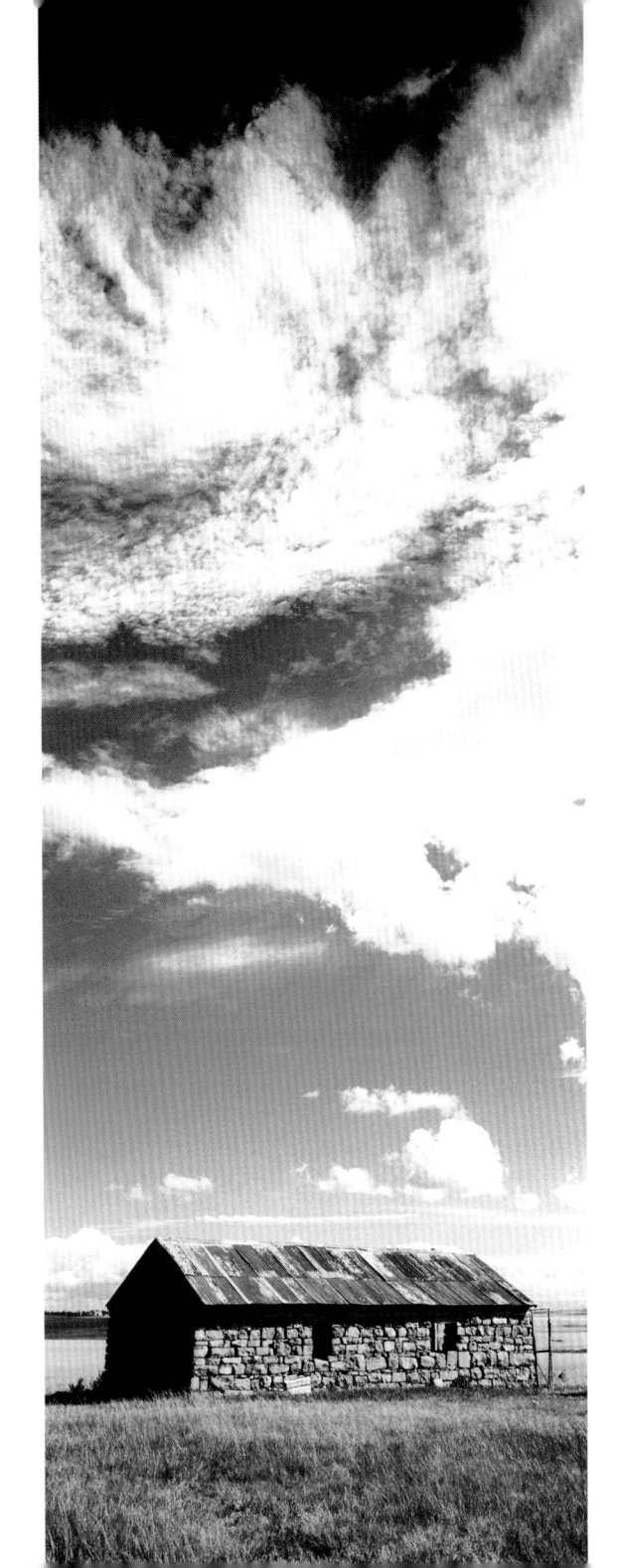

Rock is our foundation. And yet, the crust of the earth is insignificant in relation to the immense amount of material lying underneath it. The vast majority of this material, being molten, is not nearly as solid a base as we might imagine. We skate around on top of this layer picking up bits of it to make houses we think are permanent, to establish for ourselves a place to live forever. If we had the ability to see eons of time compressed into only a few minutes, however, huge boulders would disintegrate in front of our eyes and we would be left with a far better impression of the real world than we currently enjoy from our limited perspective and experience.

Page 144: Harrismith, Free State, South Africa. This page: Paarl, Western Cape, South Africa

Somerset West, Western Cape, South Africa

'When we are young we are easily influenced. As we mature we begin to choose our influences. As we grow older we realise our influence on others'

Vineyards, Western Cape, South Africa

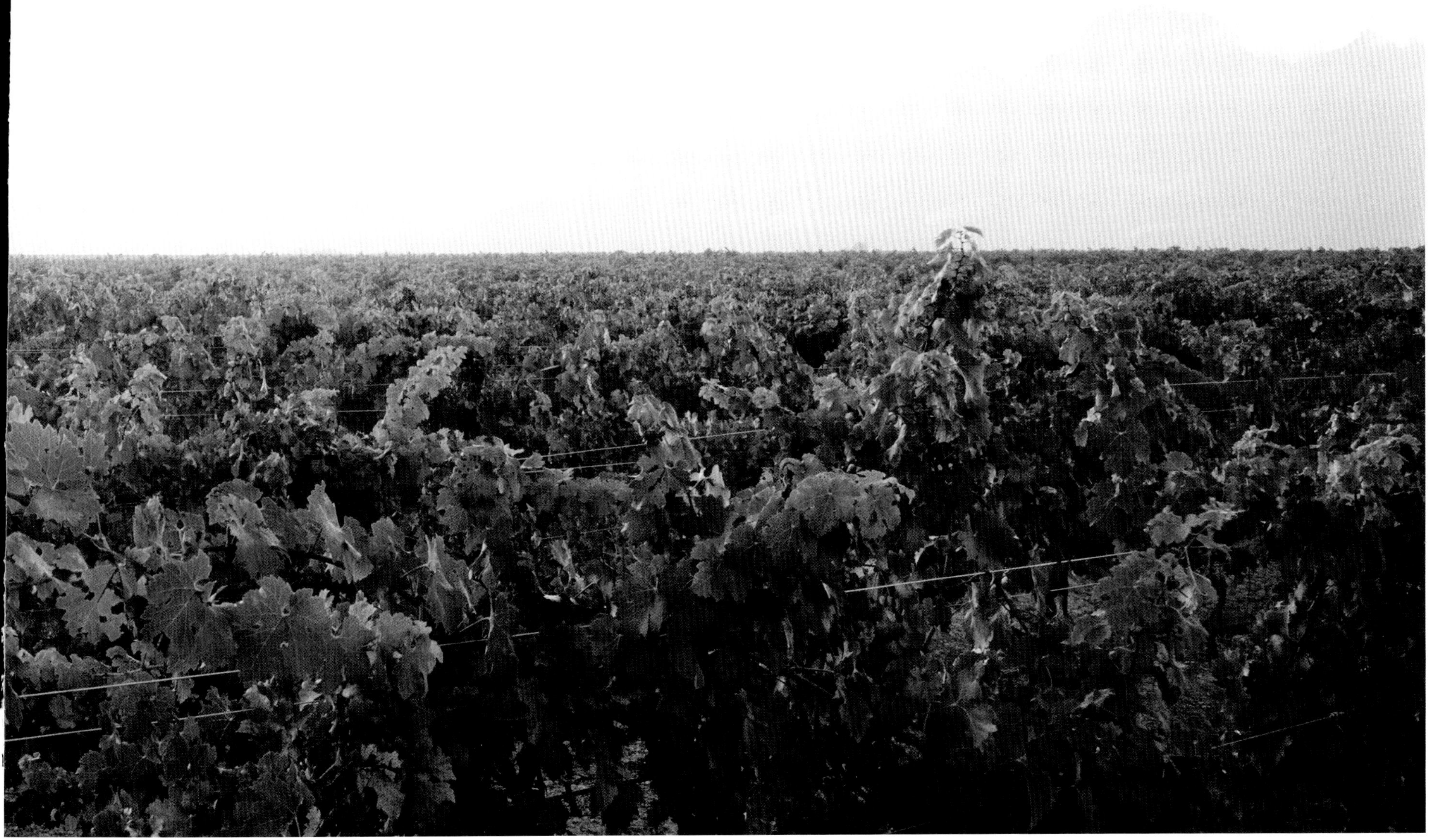

150 | Hogsback, Eastern Cape, South Africa. Following pages: Garas, Namibia

'Quite apart from the lifestyle that I enjoy through photography, I am able to savour the fact that every photograph is in itself a significant event, and it is the only event that exists for me at any one time. Indeed, any photograph may be the last event I ever experience, and so, as with everything in life I try to appreciate each image in its entirety for what it can provide'

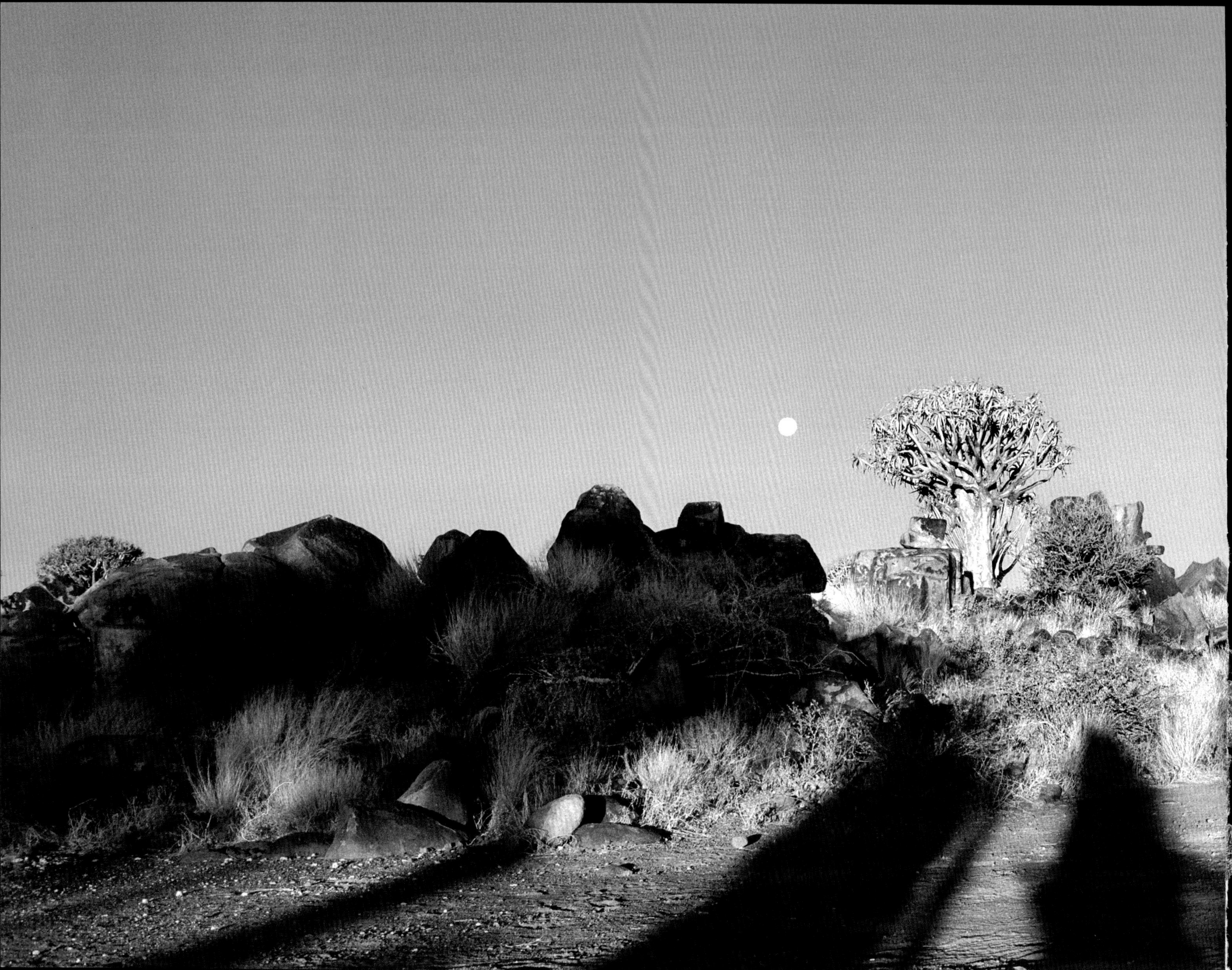

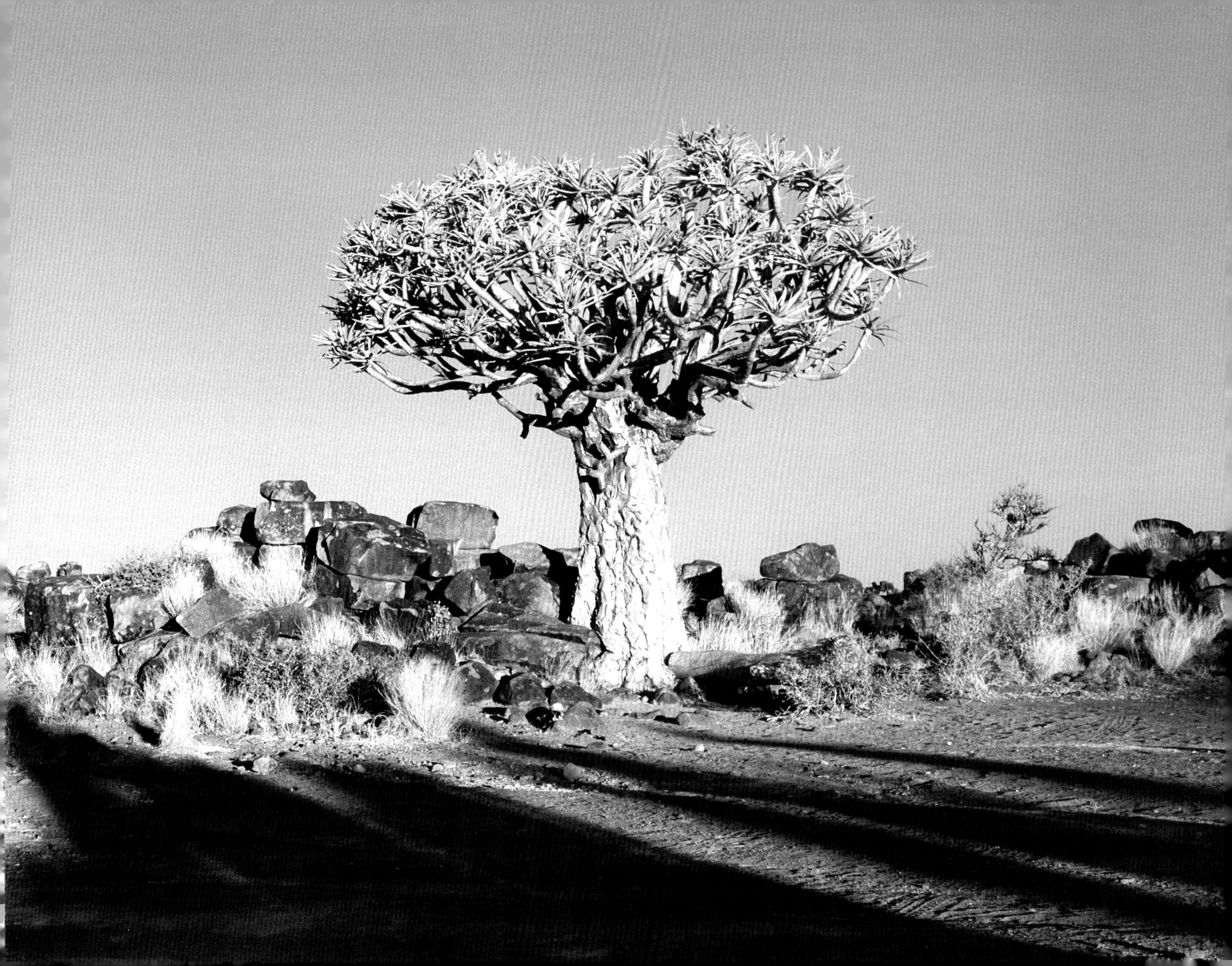

Harrismith, Free State, South Africa

KwaZulu-Natal Midlands, South Africa | 155

156 | Karoo, Western Cape, South Africa. Following pages: Kareedouw, Eastern Cape, South Africa

157

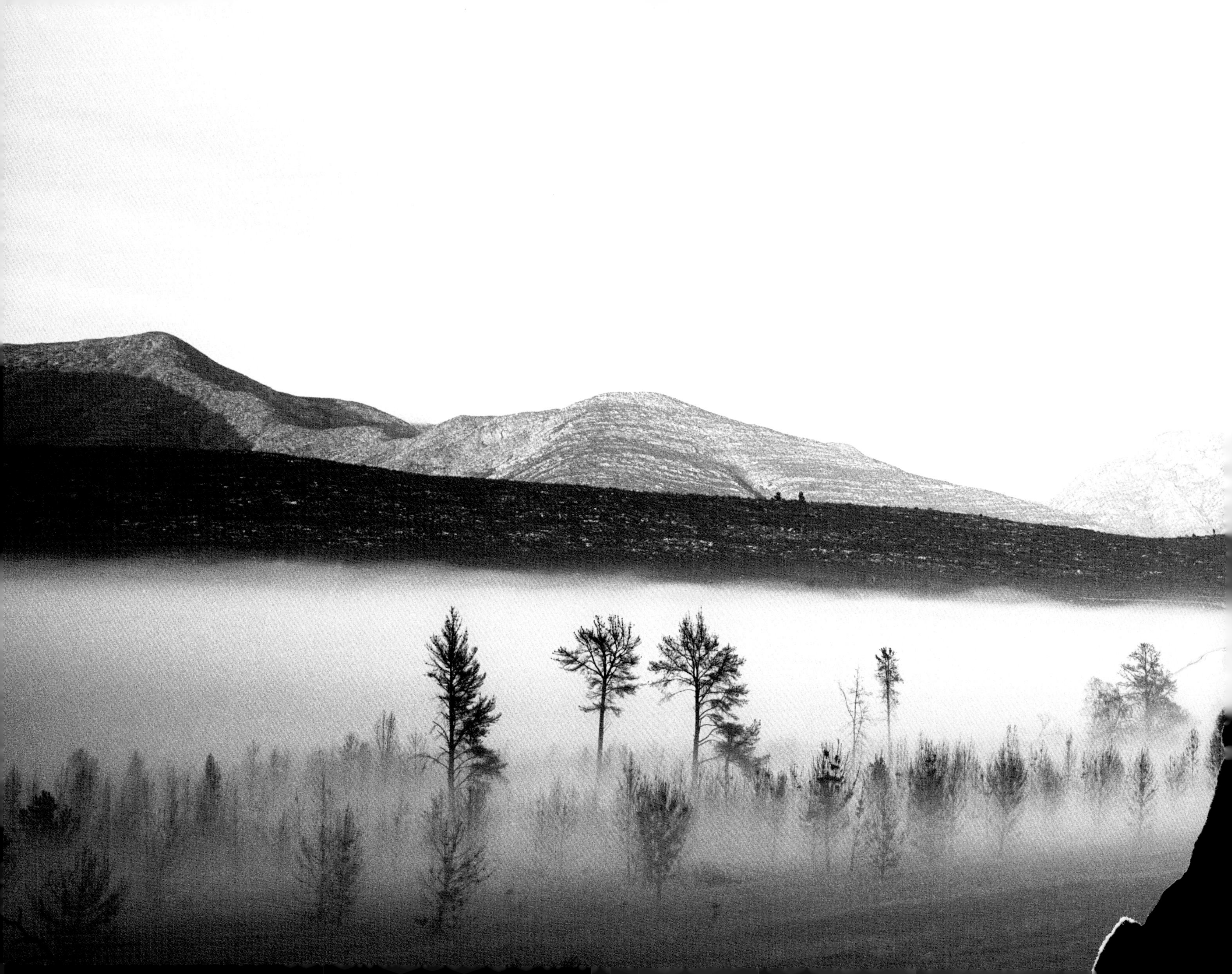

'The photograph requires nurturing also. There is a saying that it requires both a lifetime and 1/1000th of a second to take a photograph. This certainly is the case. It takes a substantial amount of time and experience, exactly the age you are now, to see the world in the way you do, so your own photograph has some significant history to it'

KwaZulu-Natal Midlands, South Africa | 161

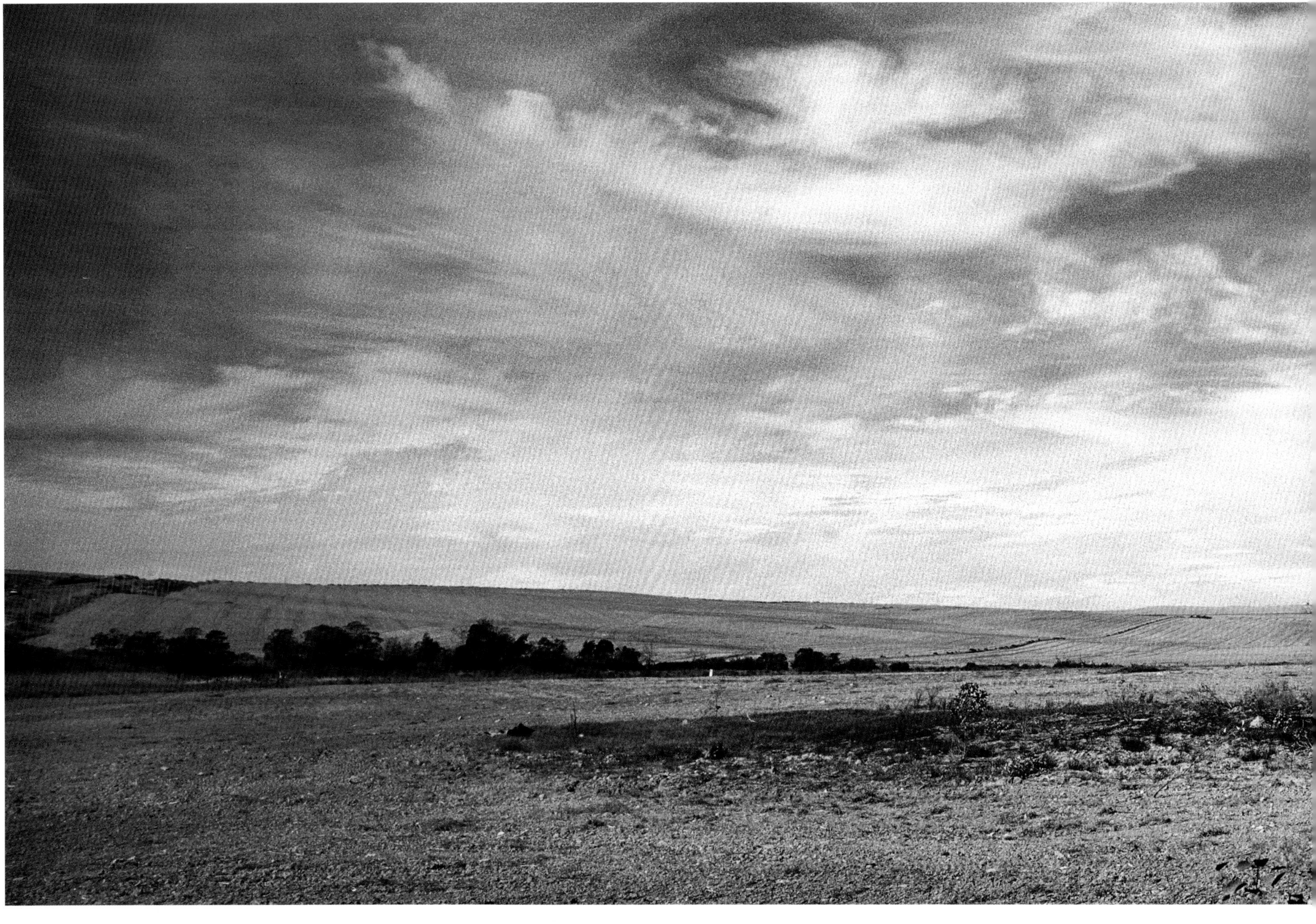

Overberg, Western Cape, South Africa | 163

164 | Karoo, Western Cape, South Africa

Our ability to read is absolutely fundamental to modern living. Reading alone is insufficient, however; it is merely a pastime, unless we use the information to move forward, to grow, and to reach our destination. Although, paradoxically, the true outcome of our lives might always remain hidden to us, reading the signs along the route helps to keep the scene in front of our eyes in clear focus. Writings become signs, signs become crossroads, and crossroads become outcomes. The outcome that we each experience today is a guide to what might lie ahead, and just as a piece of music is heard only in the present moment, this present moment is all we have.

166 | Oliviershoek, KwaZulu-Natal, South Africa. Following pages: Winberg, Free State, South Africa

'...being forced to observe, choose and communicate as we do with a landscape photograph, we are nurturing a sense of purity, wonder and contribution in ourselves'

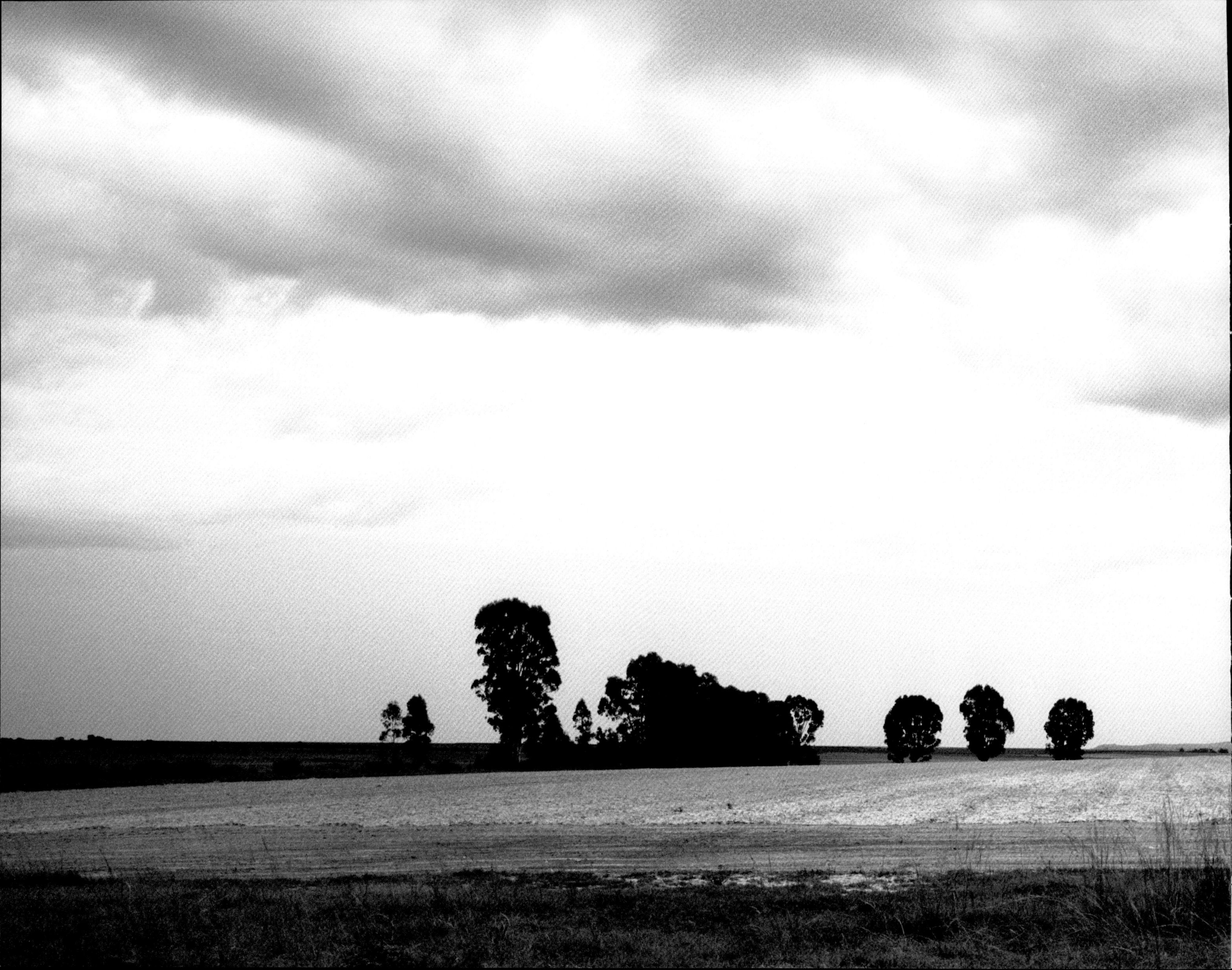

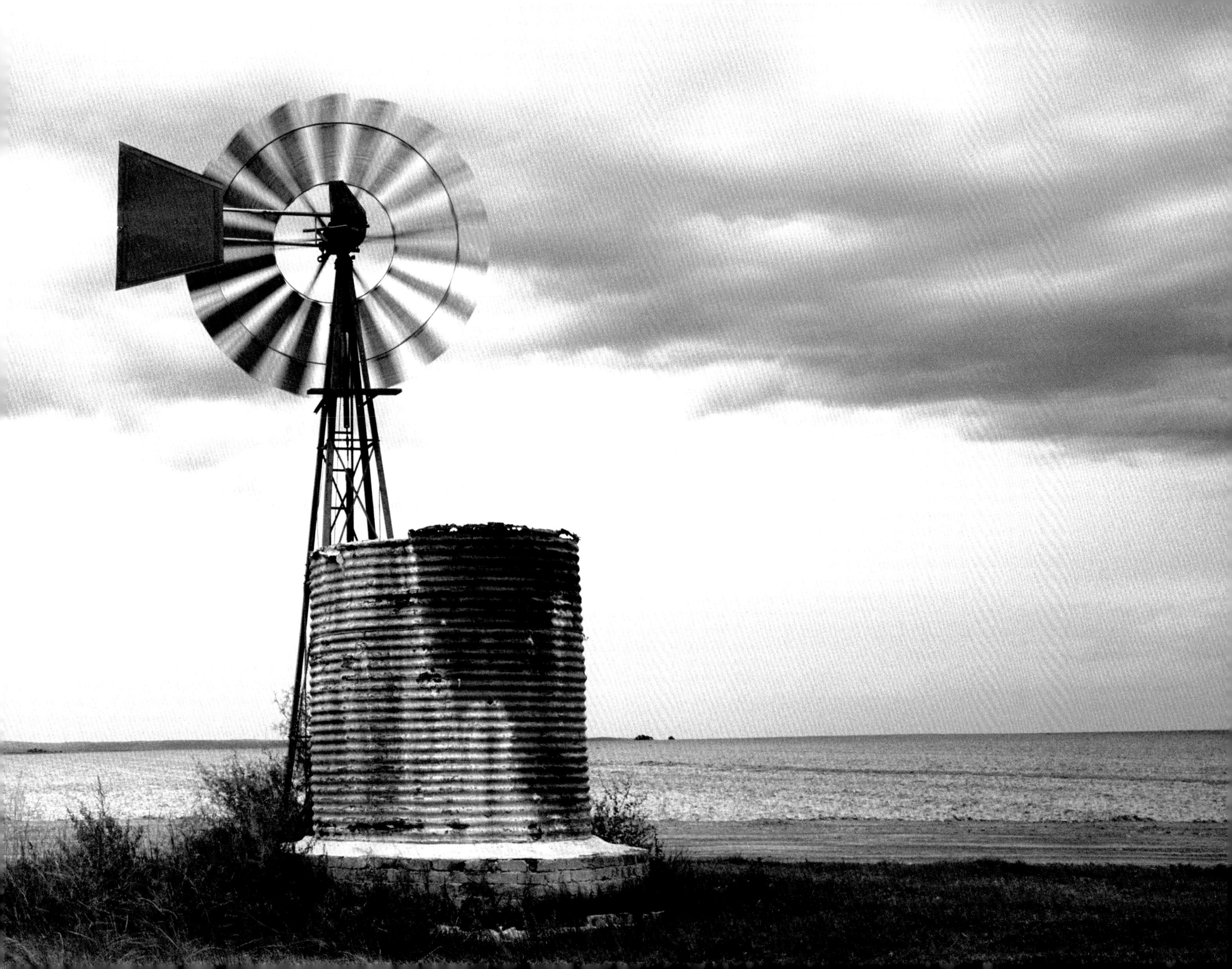

'To be a good influence one surely must have something to give. And having something to give is the best indicator of having enough yourself'

Karoo, Western Cape, South Africa | 171

KwaZulu-Natal Drakensberg, South Africa

Near Villiersdorp, Western Cape, South Africa | 173

174 | Middleberg, Karoo, Western Cape, South Africa

"Our influence over others can be positive, inspirational and loving, but we must have an awareness of this and work towards been influenced in the same way in return"

176 | Karoo, near Hex River Pass, Western Cape, South Africa

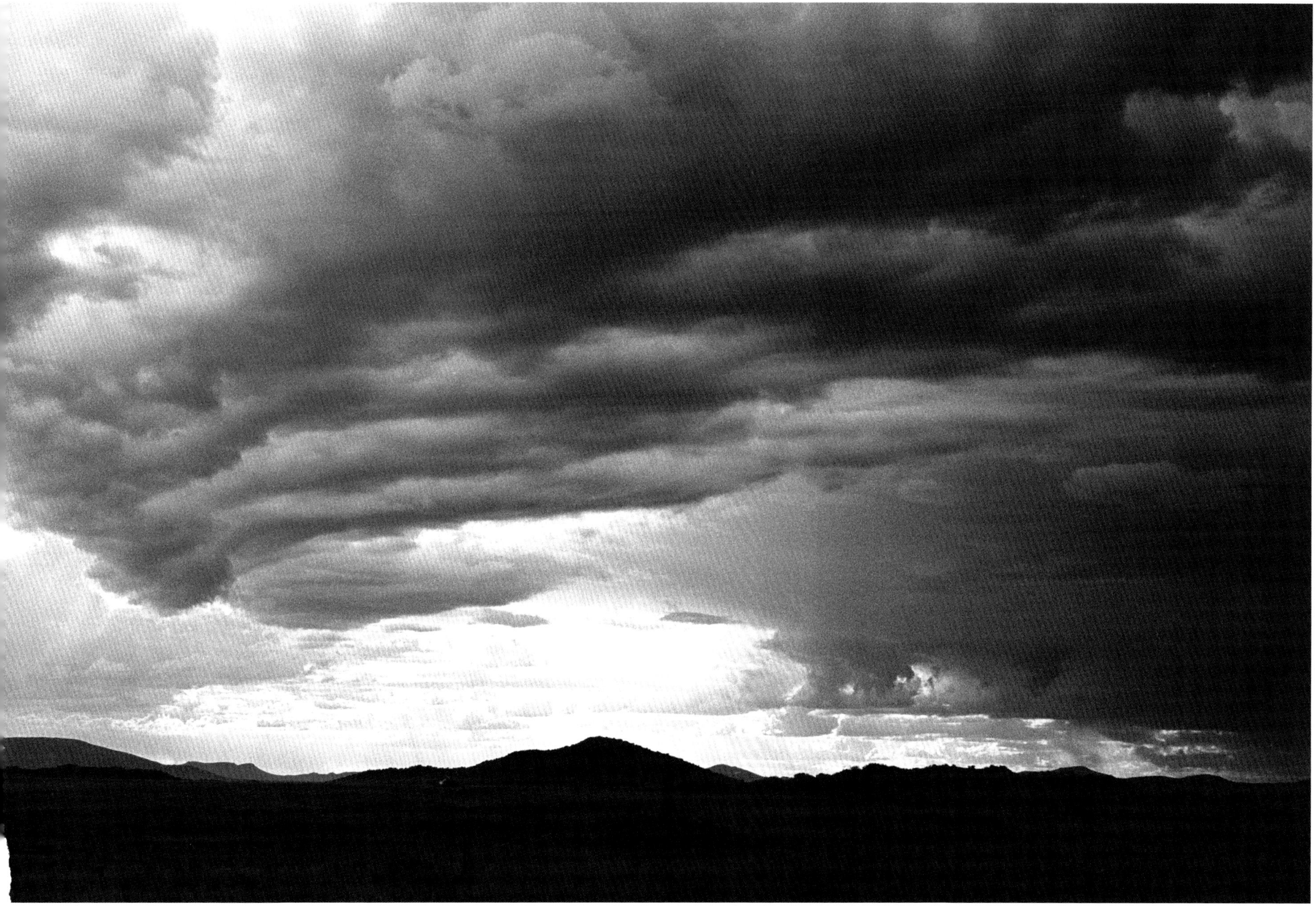

Acknowledgements

'All of you, and everyone else involved, made all the difference'

When Neil Austen telephoned me from Art Publishers with a proposal to publish a book, my fear of a thousand rejections suddenly dissipated, and I knew that the time was finally right. I want to say to everyone who encouraged me over the years to author one that they were correct, but that I am glad I waited.

Throughout the wait my family have been eternally supportive, even my children, bouncing around in the back of the Hilux down Van Zyl's Pass while colouring in and listening to songs. My parents provided a solid outdoor grounding, and I remain deeply grateful. To my friends from Johannesburg living amongst giant buildings, those from Langebaan with its giant views, and those from some very tiny places in between, you kept me (mostly) sane. You know who you are and I will value all of you forever. Everyone who has bought or complimented me on my photographs over the last twelve years has ensured that I stayed committed to this pursuit. Art Publishers, particularly John and Neil, provided guidance and dedication. Angela tirelessly applied the changes to her brilliant layout almost before I could suggest any.

All of you, and everyone else involved, made all the difference.

Author & Photographer

Bruce Mortimer grew up in South Africa, where he lives with his wife, Karen, and their three young boys Devon, Arran and Kian. Although a geologist by formal training, Bruce has followed his passion and pursued a career in fine art landscape photography since 1995.

Bruce has a minimalist approach to his work, using unsophisticated equipment and simple compositions, and combines travel and photography unobtrusively. His travels have taken him to over twenty different countries, although his portfolio of work is concentrated on South Africa, Namibia (which he has visited ten times) and Mozambique (which he has visited four times). Bruce Mortimer's Southern African photographs have been exhibited widely and hang in homes and offices throughout the world. More recently, Bruce has compiled a comprehensive portfolio of landscapes from throughout New Zealand, and continues to find pleasure in discovering places both far away and close to home. Bruce tempers his photography with numerous diverse interests, many of them contributing directly to his success as a photographer. Further examples of his work can be viewed at www.brucemortimer.com.

'Bruce has followed his passion and pursued a career in fine art landscape photography since 1995'

'I can only hope that my own photographs provide viewers with their own experience, from which they can carry something forward with them, which they can nurture and use positively in our world'

Produced by Art Publishers (Pty) Ltd
Durban, Johannesburg, Cape Town

Copyright © 2007

ISBN 1-919688-68-4

All rights reserved. No part of this publication may be reproduced in any form or transmitted in any forms or by any means, without the express permission of the author or the publishers.